Baby Steps to STEM

Other Redleaf Press Books by Jean G. Barbre

Foundations of Responsive Caregiving: Infants, Toddlers, and Twos

Activities for Responsive Caregiving: Infants, Toddlers, and Twos

Baby Steps to
STEM

Infant and Toddler Science, Technology, Engineering, and Math ACTIVITIES

Jean G. Barbre, EdD

Redleaf Press®
www.redleafpress.org
800-423-8309

Published by Redleaf Press
10 Yorkton Court
St. Paul, MN 55117
www.redleafpress.org

First edition 2017
Cover design by Jim Handrigan
Cover photograph by iStockphoto.com/ryasick
Interior design by Percolator Graphic Design
Typeset in Celeste Pro, Mr. Eaves XL Sans, and Filson Soft
Interior photographs by Shawn Patrick Thomas
Printed in the United States of America

Library of Congress Cataloging-in-Publication Data
Names: Barbre, Jean G., author.
Title: Baby steps to STEM : infant and toddler science, technology,
    engineering, and math activities / Jean G. Barbre, EdD.
Description: First edition. | St. Paul, MN : Redleaf Press, 2017. | Includes
    bibliographical references and index.
Identifiers: LCCN 2017009902 (print) | LCCN 2017023058 (ebook) | ISBN
    9781605545097 (ebook) | ISBN 9781605545080 (paperback)
Subjects: LCSH: Science–Study and teaching (Early childhood)–United States.
    | Technology–Study and teaching (Early childhood)–United States. |
    Engineering–Study and teaching (Early childhood)–United States. |
    Mathematics–Study and teaching (Early childhood)–United States. | BISAC:
    EDUCATION / Teaching Methods & Materials / Science & Technology. | FAMILY
    & RELATIONSHIPS / Life Stages / Infants & Toddlers. | EDUCATION / Teaching
    Methods & Materials / General. | EDUCATION / Curricula.
Classification: LCC LB1140.5.S35 (ebook) | LCC LB1140.5.S35 B37 2017 (print)
    | DDC 372.35/044–dc23
LC record available at https://lccn.loc.gov/2017009902

Printed on acid-free paper   U18-08

To Charlie and Carly: May you be blessed with good health, happiness, and exciting adventures.

When we treat children's play as seriously as it deserves, we are helping them feel the joy that's to be found in the creative spirit. It's the things we play with and the people who help us play that make a great difference in our lives.

—Fred Rogers

Contents

Foreword

Children are innately curious from birth—they are constantly experimenting, exploring, and discovering. In this exciting book, *Baby Steps to STEM: Infant and Toddler Science, Technology, Engineering, and Math Activities*, Jean Barbre has broken through and addresses the need in infant-toddler classrooms for a comprehensive look at the cognitive development of our youngest learners. Infant and toddler teachers have been in need of a text such as this to enrich their curriculum and offer STEM-based concepts and activities. STEM concepts have long deserved a place in the classroom next to social, emotional, art, and literacy, and yet they are often overlooked, especially in infant-toddler settings. This is a need Jean clearly recognizes.

From the beginning, Jean lays the ground work of infant-toddler development and STEM curriculum within the classroom. Going from theory to practice can be challenging for even the most seasoned teacher. Jean begins with what we know about infant and toddler development and then masterfully shows the intersection to curriculum.

The text is well researched and, at the same time, user friendly, making it a valuable resource for early childhood caregivers.

Jean recognizes the important role of the early childhood caregivers in nurturing the whole child: the social, emotional, physical, creative, and cognitive. In addition, she pays special attention to the environment, safety, and materials, showing her in-depth understanding of the challenges of the early childhood setting.

Jean has created a usable manual for early childcare providers to understand the importance of STEM theory, in addition to practical tools for them to use directly with the children. She has used her years of research and practice to assemble a collection of age-appropriate activities designed with the building blocks of STEM skills. I am excited about the potential impact this book will have in the field of infant and toddler education; it should be a staple in every program.

Susan Wood, MA
Director of the Children's Center at Caltech

Acknowledgments

First and foremost, I would like to thank the wonderful staff at Redleaf Press, including David Heath, Kara Lomen, Laurie Herrmann, Kari Cornell, and the creative team for your support and enthusiasm for *Baby Steps to STEM.* You have made this book a pleasure for me to work on. I want to thank Kimberly Bohannon for being my "coexplorer" in my STEM adventures. I am very grateful for your insights into young children and commitment to high-quality STEM learning environments. I would like to thank the amazing staff of the Orange Coast College Harry and Grace Steele Children's Center. I want to acknowledge all your efforts in preparation for the photography sessions and for allowing me to capture the beautiful children in your program. I'd like to thank the Fullerton College Child Development and Educational Studies Laboratory School. I appreciate your strong commitment to STEM-rich early learning environments. Your outdoor classroom is an enchanting place for young STEM learners. Again, thank you to both of these exceptional programs for allowing me to observe and photograph the children in your programs. A special thanks to my photographer, Shawn Thomas, for capturing the joy and excitement of the children in these two programs. I want to acknowledge Jillian Tsujimoto for helping me create the sample STEM activities needed for this book. It was fun working with you, and I wish you the best on your career path. I also want to acknowledge Peter Chang, executive director of the Child Creativity Lab, for allowing Jillian to create STEM activities in his loose parts creativity lab. I'd like to thank my family and friends for their interest in and support for this book. A special thank-you to my husband for his patience and understanding during the long hours I've spent sitting in front of my computer writing this book. Lastly, I want to acknowledge Charlie and Carly, who remind me daily of the joy and excitement of being young and discovering the world around them.

Born with a Sense of Wonder

From the moment they are born, young children are innately inquisitive and filled with a sense of wonder. They are beautiful and amazing people who delight in the simplest discovery. Each new experience provides opportunities for the children to learn about the world. They are amazed by simple things that adults often take for granted, such as watching a butterfly resting on a tree branch or rolling or bouncing a ball across the floor or smelling the sweet fragrance of a flower. Their eagerness and excitement for learning about the world makes caring for them a joy.

Consider this: Every waking hour, young children are discovering and learning new things. Infants grow and change rapidly as they transition from complete reliance on the care of others to independent toddlers who are running, jumping, and talking. The task of infants, toddlers, and twos is to make sense of the world around them, and that's just what they are busy doing each and every day. Young children are naturally curious about the world and how things work. They will touch and handle each new object with excitement and curiosity. Babies will mouth new objects and intently watch and listen to everything around them. As babies become more mobile, they will scoot or crawl over to new objects that have caught their eye. The simplest of objects, such as a rattle or sensory ball, will be of great interest to them. They may hold, mouth, and manipulate each new object to explore how it works. Toddlers and twos, on the other hand, move at rapid speed, quickly shifting from one activity to another. Whatever toddlers do, whether it's pushing shopping carts, playing dress-up, building objects, or digging in the sand, these activities are all about discovery. It's fascinating to observe infants, toddlers, and twos as they explore their surroundings. Each new exploration and discovery adds to their knowledge and understanding about the world around them.

Infants, toddlers, and twos naturally approach the world with the same curiosity required to learn and explore the foundations of science, technology, engineering, and mathematics (STEM). It is their curiosity and innate sense of wonder that inspires adults to provide optimal learning experiences for them. The care and nurturing infants, toddlers, and twos receive from adults during these formative years dramatically affects the children's future intellectual, social, emotional, and physical development. As caregivers, we have the privilege of influencing how young children acquire skills and master developmental competencies. By building positive relationships with young children and providing them with optimal play-based learning opportunities, caregivers play an important role in shaping the way those children will approach learning in the future. Those of us who work and live with young children know that each day is different. Our homes and child care centers are busy, noisy, and sometimes demanding places. Our days are full of opportunities to provide not only nurturing care for young children, but also an intentional learning environment for them. Each new experience provides children with opportunities to develop and learn skills needed for the future.

1

How Infants, Toddlers, and Twos Learn

EXPERIENTIAL LEARNING

Young children build their learning and understanding about the world through everyday play experiences. They discover how to make meaning of the world around them through hands-on experiential learning. Exploration and discovery provide endless opportunities for children to make meaningful connections and build on prior knowledge. So when does experiential STEM learning begin and how do we teach it? Experiential learning begins at birth, and in some areas of development, such as hearing, it begins prenatally. Experts tell us that auditory systems develop in utero and are fully functioning by birth. Early childhood professionals also know that children are ready to learn beginning at birth. So we ask ourselves, "If children are ready to learn, how do we as caregivers begin infants, toddlers, and twos down the path of learning STEM?" A caregiver recently said to me, "My babies are learning STEM every day!" and I completely agree. We begin to teach young children, even our youngest children, about STEM through responsive caregiving and everyday experiences beginning in infancy.

We know that babies are active learners, and they learn and explore in different ways than older children. When considering STEM learn-ing, we would never recommend introducing babies to the principles of STEM in the same way we teach older children. We introduce babies and young toddlers to STEM by talking, reading, and playing with them. We provide them with interesting age-appropriate materials to explore, and we point out to them little everyday things that are STEM related. For example, a caregiver might have a child smell a flower and talk about the petals of the flower. Or she might point out a butterfly that just landed on a leaf. Perhaps the caregiver reads a book such as *Pat the Bunny*, allowing the child to touch and feel different textures. She could plan an activity where the children are listening to different types of bells. Each bell has a different ring, providing the child with opportunities to hear the different sounds and tones. Caregivers can support the learning of infants and young toddlers by sitting in close proximity to the child and giving nonverbal gestures such as smiling or winking at the child as she plays. These nonverbal gestures communicate recognition and approval of the child's action or engagement. For now, it's important to know that babies and young toddlers are learn-ing about STEM as they actively engage with their caregivers. We also know that young children learn through sensory experiences.

Everyday sensory activities provide experiences that form the foundation for STEM learning. Let me explain. We know that babies investigate the world using their five senses. They are watching people and objects by moving their eyes, hearing sounds with their ears, tasting with their mouths, smelling with their noses, and touching with their hands and feet. Their whole bodies are taking in the world around them by using their senses. It's how babies learn. Sensory experiences introduce babies and young children to STEM. Each play experience and investigation offers a form of experiential learning. For example, we give an infant a new object, such as a wooden ring, and the first thing the child does is put it in her mouth to taste and explore it. Infants will spend a great deal of time orally exploring an object. The process of exploring an object through her senses brings a child pleasure. It is important for caregivers to provide safe, nontoxic sensory objects for a young child to explore. Using a variety of sensory objects for the child, such as things that are soft, hard, smooth, rough, bumpy, or sticky, allows the child opportunities to begin constructing new STEM knowledge. Motor development, such as kicking, pulling, and pushing, occurs as the child is discovering his world through sensory exploration. These early sensory explorations provide the foundations of learning about the physical properties of objects. This is the beginning of STEM education for young children.

As children become older and more independent, their world changes. They are able to navigate to a favorite object they see and stay focused on one activity for longer periods of time. They are able to investigate and explore through child-directed learning. Each new experience provides opportunities for building upon prior learning. Each new learning opportunity helps children reach the next developmental milestone. Responsive caregivers are knowledgeable about how children learn and provide a variety of activities and materials to support children's mastery of new skills. They provide age-appropriate opportunities for children to test out their cognitive theories. Children test out their theories daily through trial and error, repeated gestures, observations, and exploration. Toddlers and twos explore the world with the same enthusiasm as babies. They too explore the world through their senses, but their developing language and cognitive skills add to their hands-on experiential learning. As children grow older, their advancing language deepens their experiences as they communicate their needs, ask questions, and build vocabulary. Their thinking and problem-solving skills become more advanced as their brains develop.

EARLY BRAIN DEVELOPMENT

Birth to age three is a critical period when a child's brain is rapidly developing. STEM-rich activities provide opportunities to strengthen the developing brain of infants and toddlers. During the first three years of life, the brain is more flexible than during any other period of time. Throughout these early years, the brain is highly responsive to the presence or absence of experiences and to the surrounding environment. Intentional planning of STEM activities allows developing brains to take in new information and adapt to new learning with ease. The brain loves novelty, so responsive caregivers introduce new sensory materials to add interest for young children. The activities in this book are rich in sensory exploration and novel ways to stimulate brain development.

Babies are born with billions of nerve cells, or neurons. Information is stored and processed by these neurons. At the end of each neuron are dendrites that send chemical transmissions to adjoining dendrites. When information is received, it is then passed through the cells to the axons. These long, strand-like fibers are at the other end of each neuron. Axons then pass information on to nearby neurons. Although the neurons don't touch, they send a rapid chemical exchange of information from neuron to neuron. This chemical exchanged is passed across the synapse. Strengthening synaptic connections is essential to the survival of all living things. Neurons that are not stimulated go through a natural process called *synaptic pruning*. Because young children's brains are susceptible to pruning and stimulation, it is essential for brain growth and development that synaptic connections take place. When young children are exposed to a variety of rich and engaging experiences, those critical synaptic connections occur. Responsive caregivers support children's play experiences and exploration, which have the potential to strengthen the brain. STEM materials and activities offer engaging opportunities to capitalize on this period of brain development and cognitive growth.

COGNITIVE DEVELOPMENT

One of the main tasks of infants and toddlers is to make sense of their world. We know that learning begins at birth through hands-on experiences and exploration. Each new interaction or exploration has the potential to strengthen existing cognitions and elicit new learning. As children's cognitive processes develop, their thinking becomes more advanced and sophisticated. Over time, a child's cognitive abilities increase. Jean Piaget (1896–1980) theorized that children construct their own learning as they learn to make sense of the world. He recognized that children's natural curiosity motivated them to explore and investigate their environment. It is through children's active engagement with the world around them that cognitive skills are developed. STEM-rich, play-based activities and responsive caregiving provide children with opportunities to build these critical cognitive structures.

Piaget believed that children acquire and construct learning through testing out their theories and through exploration. Piaget referred to young children as "little scientists." I agree; children, like scientists, are constantly testing out their "theories." Piaget's "theories" are also referred to as *constructs*, or simply ideas. Like scientists, children test out their ideas or theories through cause and effect. Each interaction presents new learning and builds on prior knowledge. For example, a child stands at a water table for a long period, pouring water from one container to another. Here a child may have a theory of what water feels like or how water drips from one container to another. She may first fill a plastic measuring cup with water and then pour it out. Next, she may use a plastic pitcher, pouring the water out through the spout. The child may watch the water as it drips through her hands and fingers. In this example of water play, the young child is stimulating her senses as she sees, feels, and hears the water splashing and running through her hands and is learning about the physical properties of water as well as gravity, quantity, and volume. The child is testing out her theory about water and water play, forming new ideas or schemas.

A *schema* can be defined as a set of linked mental representations of the world, which we use both to understand and to respond to situations. As they form schemas, children organize knowledge around a group of ideas or components. Piaget emphasized the importance of schemas in cognitive development. Here is an example of how a young child might develop a life science schema about rabbits. A classroom has a pet rabbit. A young child observes the rabbit hopping or eating. The teacher helps the infant or toddler gently stroke the rabbit's fur, saying, "Soft touch." The teacher points out how the rabbit wiggles its nose, and has whiskers and large upright ears. When a child is able to walk, he goes over to the rabbit to observe it more closely. The caregiver might say, "This is where the rabbit lives. It's the rabbit's habitat." Over time, the child has learned that the rabbit is "our class pet," and we treat it gently and with respect. Each interaction strengthens the child's knowledge and understanding of the physical characteristics of rabbits and their habitat. In

this example, the child is learning a lot about life science and where a rabbit lives, how it moves, the feel of its fur, how its nose wiggles, and what it eats. Each experience builds on prior knowledge and content and helps the child construct groups of ideas or schemas. It is important for young children to play and explore with a variety of living and nonliving objects and materials. It is through these play experiences that young children begin to form schemas that are necessary for STEM learning. Experiential learning builds and stimulates the developing brain and advances cognitive development.

According to Piaget's theory, there are four stages of cognitive development: sensorimotor, preoperational, concrete operations, and formal operations. The first stage, sensorimotor, occurs from birth to age two. During this stage, infants begin exploring their world through sensory and motor experiences. By the end of this stage, two-year-old children are beginning to construct learning through mental representations and sensorimotor experiences. As children reach age two, they enter what Piaget calls the preoperational stage. In this stage, children use symbols, including words, features, pictures, and models, to represent objects and events (Dodge, Rudick, and Berke 2006). Language begins to develop during the preoperational period along with the

in the formal operational stage, children's thinking becomes more logical and abstract. The first two stages, sensorimotor and preoperational, have relevance for adults caring for children birth to age three.

The young children in your care are busy constructing knowledge during the sensorimotor and preoperational stages. The more intentional the activities and play experiences are, the richer a child's learning becomes. Repeating and varying the experiences over time allows children to build upon prior learning and construct deeper and more complex thinking. The following example of the use of bubbles in the classroom illustrates the stages of cognitive development.

beginning of reasoning skills and the constant "Why?" questions. During the concrete operational stage, children ages seven to eleven are developing more logical reasoning skills, yet they are not able to think at an abstract level. Finally,

- *Young infants.* A young infant may just watch and observe the colors of the bubbles. The caregiver would explain that bubbles float and allow the child to feel the wetness of the bubbles.

PIAGET'S FOUR STAGES OF COGNITIVE DEVELOPMENT

Stage	Age	Cognitive tasks
Sensorimotor	Birth to two years	Infants learn about the world with their eyes, ears, hands, and mouths. Infants use sensorimotor skills to begin solving problems. They develop object permanence and are beginning to understand properties of objects around them.
Preoperational	Two to seven years	Children use symbols, such as numbers and words, to represent earlier sensorimotor discoveries. The development of language allows children to engage in pretend play with others. Their developing language and thinking prompts them to ask "Why?" as they learn and make sense of the world.
Concrete operational	Seven to eleven years	Children's reasoning becomes more logical but is still based in concrete experiences. They are focused on the here and now. Children understand that actions can be reversed.
Formal operational	Eleven years and up	Adolescents have the capacity to think about abstract concepts and other people's ideas. This allows them to think systematically, form hypotheses, and reason deductively about possible real-world situations. This thinking is important for long-term planning and consideration of possible outcomes and consequences of actions.

- *Older infants.* As the child gets older, the caregiver would assist the child as she dips the wand into the soapy water. The caregiver would model how to blow into the wand and then let the child try blowing. The caregiver might comment to the child, "Look at the bubbles! See how the wind catches the bubble? See all the colors too!" The caregiver would talk about the way the bubbles move in the wind, the different sizes of the bubbles, and how they "pop." He might say, "Oh, they pop and disappear!" All of these interactions are introducing the child to the areas of STEM.

- *Young toddlers.* A toddler who has the developmental skills to handle the wand by himself may experiment with the way in which bubbles are formed by moving and swinging the wand. Here the child is learning the principles of physical science: motion, speed, and gravity. Throughout these activities, the caregiver would describe the activity and help build the child's vocabulary and understanding of additional concepts such as big, little, high, low, floating, wet, round, and shiny.

- *Toddlers and twos.* With prior experience and knowledge, the older toddler could take the soapy water and wand outside and explore on her own. A caregiver might have the children construct or engineer their own wands (see Bubble Wands activity, page 66) out of chenille stems (also called pipe cleaners) or wire hangers. A caregiver would document the child's experience and note it in her anecdotal records. The child could draw a picture of the bubble activity, and the teacher could record how the child describes her play experience. The teacher could help the child continue building her vocabulary and use of language through this STEM activity.

As children reach two years of age, they enter into the preoperational stage. This stage, which lasts until approximately age seven, is characteristic of children's growing ability to use and manipulate objects, words, and drawings in a way

that represents their new cognitive abilities. The preoperative stage shows a growing mastery over mental reasoning and the development of magical beliefs. During this period, there is growing interest in reasoning and wondering why things happen. We observe this period in the older two- and three-year-old who is constantly asking the question "Why?" Knowing this questioning period is a normal stage of cognitive development helps caregivers respond positively to seemingly endless Why questions by the child. During this period, young children are beginning to develop more advanced thinking and reasoning skills as they learn to make sense of their world.

During the preoperational stage, children also begin to engage in pretend play. With a growing ability to manipulate their environment and an expanding vocabulary, young children use objects and mental representations to expand and test out their learning. During this period, older toddlers begin to interact and play with peers in more cooperative and pretend play. For example, several children may build a structure using cardboard boxes and imagine it to be a spaceship. In the block area, children may use the blocks and ramps and create a racetrack, using the cars and materials in a symbolic way. Using this example, we may see an older toddler extend her play by making the sound "vroom vroom vroom" to mimic the sound of the car racing down the ramp. Symbolic play demonstrates how the child is developing a foundation of abstract thinking. This stage lays the groundwork for more advanced cognitive skills. The development of abstract thought and problem solving is based in the sensorimotor and preoperational stages of cognitive development. These skills are needed to prepare children for the twenty-first century. Cognitive development provides the foundation for all STEM learning.

THE IMPORTANCE OF PLAY

Play is the business of childhood. Children learn and grow through play. During play, young children are engaging both their minds and bodies. Children use small and large muscles as they move and manipulate objects. Through play children integrate emotions, solve problems, learn language, and develop their imaginations. They learn how to interact and communicate with others. It's important to remember that children's play will look different at different ages. For example, an infant's style of play looks different than toddler play. Play is not something children automatically know how to do, but rather it is an activity that is learned through playful engagement with others. Responsive caregivers join children in their play experiences and encourage exploration and enjoyment in play. Responsive caregivers promote a child's natural curiosity as they model and scaffold play. They help foster relationships with peers and promote development.

Play begins in infancy as babies and caregivers build early relationships. Babies imitate the gestures and expressions of adults. Through play, infants and toddlers develop confidence in their ability to manipulate the world. They build cognitive skills that support STEM learning, including cause and effect, memory, and spatial awareness. When observing infants and toddlers, caregivers watch them learn through sensory exploration, manipulation, and trial and error. Infants spend

most of their playtime playing alone or with a responsive caregiver, but as children grow, they become more aware of others. They begin to observe the play and interactions of others. As they begin to pay closer attention to those around them, they move into parallel play. As children grow and mature, their language, cognitive, and motor skills increase, and they begin to move toward cooperative play. Children approaching their third birthday will use their developing imaginations and social skills to play with others in pretend and cooperative play.

Caregivers promote cognitive development by planning intentional, developmentally appropriate activities. Cognitive thinking and play experiences are important for early development. Children spend most of their time in play where they construct new learning and develop critical thinking skills. When caregivers provide a rich STEM environment, children can direct and design their own play. In child-directed play, unless an activity is harmful or destructive, children are allowed to play freely. Infants and toddlers will repeat simple activities in order to master new skills. For example, a child picks up a sensory bottle and twists and shakes it to see how the objects in it move and float (see Liquid Sensory Bottles activity, page 108). Caregivers watch and observe the child, providing support and guidance in a developmentally appropriate manner. They scaffold STEM learning by reinforcing new vocabulary and expanding language and learning through inquiry. Asking open-ended questions provides opportunities to hold a child's attention, shows approval of the child's choice of play, and increases the child's sense of self and self-esteem. I will share more on inquiry later in the book. Child-directed activities strengthen the adult-child relationship, reinforce learning, and enhance the feeling that learning is fun.

Experienced caregivers are sensitive to play responses of children. They understand that each child has distinct preferences in the amount and intensity of play. Caregivers develop an understanding of the cues infants and toddlers give when they feel under- or overstimulated. Caregivers show care and respect to the child by modifying the environment to meet the changing needs and cues of each child. Responsive caregivers talk to children about what they are doing and ask open-ended questions. Using words and gestures helps children connect prior learning to new experiences. Caregivers broaden children's learning by scaffolding STEM activities and introducing new learning materials to the play experience. Novel toys and materials are introduced, allowing children to extend their play experiences. These connections help children deepen and expand their learning and understanding of the world.

Adults have their own playful styles, and infants and toddlers quickly learn to identify the different styles of their parents and caregivers. It's important for early childhood providers to support parents in their role as their child's first teacher. Helping parents engage in play with their children promotes positive relationships and helps children reach developmental milestones. Playful environments at home and in early care settings provide a consistent message that learning is fun. It supports the home-school connec-

tion, which is so important for children's learning. Children spend most of their time in play where they construct new learning; therefore, play is essential in high-quality early care centers. Caregivers can do the following to support STEM play activities in young children:

- Talk to the child as you play.

- Model how to play and use animated expressions.

- Ask inquiry questions and introduce STEM vocabulary.

- Provide children space to play and explore alone and with peers.

- Scaffold the activity by modeling expanded use of the play material(s).

- Provide open-ended materials in both inside and outside environments.

- Join the child on the floor as you engage in playful activities.

- Provide toys with varying levels of difficulty across the domains, including puzzles and items for counting, sorting, and categorizing.

- Introduce new toys slowly into the center, adding novelty to the play experience.

- Talk about the activity to help children make connections to prior learning.

- Provide parents with ways to support the home-school connection.

Play provides young children with ways to develop skills and competencies across the learning domains. Social-emotional skills are developed as children engage in play with peers. They learn cooperative skills such as sharing, taking turns, managing emotions, and developing patience through play. These skills are essential for the development of the whole child. Play provides opportunities for integrated learning across the domains of cognitive, language, physical, and social development. Play provides infants and toddlers with experiences that help them learn STEM every day.

LANGUAGE DEVELOPMENT

Learning language is a universal task of children birth to age three. Language supports children's understanding of STEM. Language allows us to formulate thoughts, solve problems, and understand our world. It helps us communicate with others and express our thoughts and feelings. Learning language and how to communicate is an important part of socialization and how we collaborate with others. Responsive caregivers are intentional in the language they use to help children connect words and concepts to their creative play experiences. Language helps children put words to what they are seeing and experiencing. As children play and explore their world, language sets the stage for learning about the principles and concepts of STEM.

Language development is a dynamic process. Responsive caregivers look for opportunities to

scaffold language development through active engagement. Responsive caregivers help build children's language skills by introducing new vocabulary, asking open-ended questions, giving prompts, and modeling appropriate social use of language. It is the give-and-take between two or more people. Language is learned through the stages of receptive and expressive language. Receptive language is the ability to listen and understand what is being communicated. At birth, infants prefer the sound of adult voices to other noises. Babies are watching and listening to everything around them. Reciprocal interactions between caregivers and young children have a profound impact on the child's development of language. Positive interactions with caregivers strengthen the brain's ability to learn language and promote the child's ability to build language skills. As children listen to the words and sounds around them, their brains are actively making cognitive structures and strengthening neural connections. Expressive language begins as babies first begin to coo and babble. These early forms of communication lay the foundation of expressive language. With time, practice, and maturation, early sounds become simple words.

Later, expressive language develops into more recognized speech and language. Research shows that early exposure to language results in greater language proficiency. Responsive caregivers can help build neural connections in the brain and enhance language development by talking, singing, reading, and playing with infants and toddlers throughout the day.

Language-rich environments help young children learn language. Responsive caregivers model social use of language through self-talk and parallel talk. Self-talk is the act or practice of saying out loud what *you are thinking to yourself*. In self-talk, adults verbalize what they are seeing, hearing, and doing when caring for a young child. For example, a caregiver sitting with a young child who is playing with stacking cups might say, "I see you picking up each cup one by one. I see you stacking the cups together." A caregiver might say to an older child playing at a sensory table, "I see you using your hands and fingers to find the toys. I see you found the red car. The cornmeal is falling through your fingers." In self-talk, the caregiver states simply what she is doing. For example, a caregiver might say, "I'm going to shake this sensory bottle. I see bubbles forming. I see the balls now floating to the bottom of the bottle." Self-talk helps children begin to make connections between what they are seeing, doing, and hearing with the real world. It introduces children to vocabulary and beginning concept words. It is recommended that you don't interject open-ended questions into self-talk. There will be many other opportunities to ask questions. The goal here is for you to model what you are seeing, hearing, and watching the child do. Again, use simple sentence structure, modeling social use of language, grammar, and proper sentence formation.

Parallel talk is another way in which you can promote language development in young children. Parallel talk is similar to self-talk, but in parallel talk you are talking about what *the child is seeing, doing, and hearing*. While engaging with a baby, you might say to a child lying on an activity mat or under a cradle gym, "You just kicked the butterfly with your foot. Oh, the butterfly is moving." To an older child, you might say, "Oh, you put those blocks on top of each other. You're stacking them up high! Oops, they all fell down." Language is developed in children as the caregiver actively engages and models language. Each form of talk, self-talk or parallel, supports language development through verbalization of what you are thinking and observing in young children. Each engagement helps children build vocabulary and learn more about the world. All of these actions promote children's understanding of STEM concepts.

Connecting Words with Real-World Knowledge

Children's growing vocabulary reflects their understanding of concept words. STEM concepts such as cause and effect, push, pull, motion, and space can easily be seen in an infant-toddler environment. As children begin to understand these concepts, caregivers can help them connect the concepts with words through self-talk and parallel talk. For example, during block play, a child builds or engineers a ramp. The child then moves the cars over or under the ramp. A caregiver might say, "You've built a ramp for the cars to move over and under. See how fast the cars roll down the ramp!" We know that blocks and toy cars are materials found in almost all early care environments. Here the caregiver has simply identified the STEM concept words *build*, *move*, *over*, *under*, *fast*, and *roll* that occurred in a natural play experience. This example shows that STEM concepts can be reinforced easily in our early childhood classrooms. As I said earlier, you're probably doing lots of STEM already in your early learning environment.

It's important to expand your thinking to intentionally include STEM concepts into your everyday conversations with children. STEM activities help children deepen their understanding of basic concept words. Your job, as a responsive caregiver, is to help children develop concept words through their everyday interactions and classroom activities. Here is a list of STEM concept words that can easily be incorporated into your everyday conversations and engagement with infants, toddlers, and twos:

- over
- under
- around
- through
- up
- down
- in
- out
- between
- together
- move
- roll
- slide
- push
- fast
- slow
- force
- sink
- float
- texture
- rough
- smooth
- slippery
- sticky
- size
- shape
- form
- measurement
- height
- weight
- heavy
- light
- balance
- absorption
- reflection

Children are naturally curious. "Why?" is the question that dominates the language of children two to three years of age. Because they are naturally curious, they want to know the names of objects and how they work. For example, a child observes a caterpillar crawling on the grass. With a curious look on her face, the toddler points to the caterpillar. Her caregiver might say, "Veronica, I see you found a caterpillar. Look at it crawling slowly across the grass." The caregiver might extend the conversation and STEM learning by saying, "The caterpillar eats leaves. Let's watch his legs move." In this example, a young toddler may be just watching and observing the caterpillar. This would be developmentally appropriate for a child this age. But an older toddler or three-year-old with more expressive language skills may ask the caregiver a series of Why questions: "Why does it crawl?" or "Why does it eat leaves?" Each explanation from a caregiver may be followed by another "Why?" Responsive caregivers provide many opportunities to support children's natural curiosity. They help answer their questions, build vocabulary, and teach them additional STEM concept words.

Further, as their vocabulary increases, children begin connecting words together in two-word phrases. Through language-rich activities, children are learning new words as their comprehension of language continues to develop. Reading, talking, and singing are primary activities in high-quality early care and are seen as promoting language development in infants and toddlers. Caregivers who intentionally plan language-rich environments are setting the stage for a child to build vocabulary, enjoy playing with sounds, and use words. Caregivers can support early language development in infants and young toddlers in the following ways:

- Talk and sing to babies.

- Intentionally introduce new vocabulary and concept words.

- Use simple sentences in self-talk and parallel talk.

- Pause and take turns when talking.

- Talk slowly and intentionally.

- Engage children in the give-and-take exchange in which they talk and you listen.

- Identify the objects they see used in play.

- Talk to them as they play indoors and outdoors.

- Introduce STEM concepts in natural settings.

- Ask open-ended questions and give children time to respond.

- Offer verbal prompts to enhance the play and language development.

- Read both fiction and nonfiction books to children.

Building STEM Vocabulary

Young children learn vocabulary and the rules of language through exposure to language, music, and books. Young children build vocabulary through active involvement in storytelling. Dialogic reading is a form of reading where children are actively engaged in the reading activity. Children become involved in the reading activity by asking and answering questions and turning the pages of the book. Their interest in print grows as they make connections between the things they see and experience and the words and vocabulary they hear. Best practices recommend that you read both fiction and nonfiction books to young children. Books not only provide opportunities for young children to learn facts about STEM, but they also engage the children's imagination in the storytelling.

Children's books, both fiction and nonfiction, are a wonderful way to introduce children to the principles of STEM. Children learn factual information from nonfiction books. For example, books such as *Food from Farms* and *Farm Machines,* both by Nancy Dickmann, provide factual information about the food grown on farms and the machines used for farming. Read nonfiction books that follow children's natural interests. For example, if you see large trucks on your walk outdoors, afterward read a book like *My Big Truck Book* by Roger Priddy. Following children's interests will help deepen their knowledge and understanding of the world. Adding fiction books, in this case *Goodnight, Goodnight, Construction Site* by Sherri Rinker, engages children in the storytelling and imagination process.

Fiction books are created to inspire the imagination. Fictional stories are open to interpretation and may have some historical or factual references. STEM concepts can be found embedded in the text of many fictional children's books. One example is the classic children's story *Goldilocks and the Three Bears*. This fictional story has elements of both science and math embedded into the text. As Goldilocks first tastes the porridge she says, "This porridge is too hot!" and then goes on to say, "This porridge is too cold!" When tasting the last porridge, she says, "Ah, this porridge is just right." Here Goldilocks is learning about temperature, which is physical science. Goldilocks then learns about number sense and size as she explores the three different-size chairs. First she says, "This chair is too big!" and then she says, "This chair is too big too." As she tries the last chair she says, "Ah, this chair is just right." But just as she sits in the last chair, it breaks into tiny pieces. This story provides you with examples of how STEM principles can be found easily in most storybooks. Once you understand more about STEM, it will be easy for you to connect STEM principles and concepts with some of your favorite children's books.

Board books and soft cloth books are recommended for infants and toddlers. It's easy for little hands to help turn the pages, and the size and scale of the pages are perfect for this age child. Board books such as *My Big Animal Book* offer infants and toddlers the beginning foundation of life science and understanding the characteristics of animals, including dogs, cats, farm and jungle animals, and birds. Books that provide children with opportunities to touch and feel different materials offer them different physical properties to explore, such as rough, smooth, soft, and sticky. Books such as *Baby Touch and Feel: Animals*, *Baby Touch and Feel: Puppies and Kittens*, and *Baby Touch and Feel: Colors and Shapes* introduce infants and toddlers to a wide variety of early STEM concepts. At the back of this book is a comprehensive list of fiction and nonfiction children's STEM books. Each activity in this book includes a list of books to support and enhance STEM learning about the particular topic. It is recommended that you have a wide variety of books available in your classroom. Along with books, high-quality early learning environments provide children with developmentally appropriate materials to support STEM learning.

2

The Role of the Caregiver

Infants, toddlers, and twos are born ready to learn and are eager and excited about learning. As caregivers, we play a critical role in influencing how young children acquire skills and master developmental competencies during these formative years. Your responsive care and nurturing relationships with the children are the building blocks for lifelong learning. Your role as caregiver is to support each individual child's learning and to provide optimal learning opportunities in a loving, nurturing environment. STEM education is a key component in children's learning experiences and helps prepare them for the twenty-first century. Each new exploration and discovery adds to their overall knowledge and understanding about the world around them. Helping children learn the concepts of STEM, build vocabulary, and make home-to-school connections all support STEM learning. Intentional activities that focus on STEM add to a child's overall development. Each new experience provides children with opportunities to develop and learn skills needed for the future.

RESPONSIVE CAREGIVING

In this book, the terms *caregiver, responsive caregiver,* and *early care provider* will be used interchangeably. Responsive caregivers are those

individuals who teach and care for children while attending to their individual needs in a warm, nurturing, and loving manner. Providing responsive care is an awesome responsibility. It is imperative that responsive caregivers be sensitive to the developing child and provide opportunities to learn through play in a caring, nurturing environment. Caregivers' interactions with children should be positive and respectful and demonstrate a genuine interest in the child's well-being. In high-quality early learning centers, caregivers form strong partnerships with parents and engage them in supporting the child's learning at home.

We know that parents are the child's first teacher. Studies on the home-school connection substantiate the important role parents play in supporting their children's learning. Studies report that supportive families, no matter what their income level, have children who show greater academic success, have better social skills, and display improved classroom behavior (Henderson and Mapp 2002). You will see that each of the activities in this book contains a home-school connection. This will provide you with opportunities to assist parents in supporting their child's learning at home. Responsive caregivers also honor diversity and support each child's home language and cultural background. Throughout this book, I will be referring to different ages of children from birth to two years of age. Because

such a wide range of mastery exists within each age group, early childhood professionals define the ages and stages for children birth to age two in various ways. In this book, I identify children's age groups in the following way:

- Young infant: Birth to six months

- Older infant: Six to twelve months

- Young toddler: Twelve to twenty-four months

- Older toddler / two-year-old: Twenty-four months to thirty-six months

Responsive caregivers are knowledgeable about the ages and stages of children's development. They provide a loving, nurturing, stable, and responsive learning environment for all children. Caring for our youngest children takes a commitment and dedication from early childhood professionals who choose to work with them. As an early childhood professional, your role in pro-

viding quality care is essential to the well-being and future development of children birth to age two. As early childcare providers, we know that learning begins with responsive caregiving and nurturing relationships where play is central to children's learning. We will explore play and its important role in children's learning throughout this book.

It is our job as responsive caregivers to engage, nurture, and prepare children for the future and our rapidly changing world. The learners in your care today will be the leaders of tomorrow. How do we as infant and toddler caregivers prepare young children for the twenty-first century? What are the skills and knowledge children will need in the future? This book will provide caregivers with age-appropriate science, technology, engineering, and math activities for young children. These play-based activities are designed to start children down the path of preparing for the future.

PREPARING TWENTY-FIRST-CENTURY LEARNERS

The information age, sometimes called the digital or media age, has greatly influenced and changed our society. Technology is everywhere, and a wide range of information is at our fingertips. We communicate and share information faster than ever before. With new technology, many of our traditional ways of communicating, conducting business, manufacturing, and sharing information has changed. Technology has provided us with tools to navigate life at rapid speed. Futurists predict that new innovations and technology will continue to evolve in ways we can't even imagine, both enhancing and replacing many of the jobs and products we currently depend on.

How does this impact infants and toddlers, and why is it important that we focus on STEM in the early years? As caregivers, we must prepare the children in our care for the future by instilling in them a love for STEM and the readiness skills necessary for college and career. According to the National Education Association (NEA, accessed 2015), strengthening our nation's STEM workforce is essential in order to stay competitive in a rapidly changing global economy. It is projected that STEM occupations will grow faster than any other occupations. According to the United States Bureau of Labor Statistics, occupations related to STEM are projected to grow to more than 9 million by 2022 (National Science Foundation 2015).

As educators, we are preparing young children for jobs that have yet to be created. To do this, we must prepare ourselves to be knowledgeable and confident in the principles and practice of STEM. Throughout this book, you will see that the terms *principles* and *concepts* of STEM are used frequently and interchangeably. Principles and concepts of STEM refer to knowledge, conceptual understandings, and critical-thinking skills needed to study STEM subjects. Understanding and being confident in the principles of STEM is essential for educators and caregivers as they work and prepare young children for the future.

National and statewide initiatives have been developed to strengthen our educational system in the areas of STEM. Many are designed to encourage women, persons with disabilities, and minorities to enter STEM-related fields. One of these initiatives is the Next Generation Science Standards (NGSS, accessed 2015). The NGSS were developed through a state-led collaborative process. The new K–12 science standards, rich in content and practice, are designed across academic disciplines to prepare students for college and careers. The goal of these STEM initiatives is to prepare all students to be competent in all areas of STEM and to be prepared for the global challenges of the future. Professional development for educators is another important component in advancing STEM skills among children. Teachers and caregivers of infants through high-school-age students need to know the principles and practices of STEM. As we look ahead for the children in our care, we must ask ourselves, "How do we prepare them for the global society of the future?" and "What are the skills children will need to be college and career ready?"

The Four Cs

Along with STEM education, experts across the country identified four core skills that promote children's readiness for the twenty-first century. These skills, often referred to as the Four Cs, include critical thinking, communication, collaboration, and creativity (NEA, accessed 2016). The Four Cs are believed to promote higher-level thinking skills, ingenuity, and innovative thinking, while deepening the skills experts believe are needed to promote careers in a global society.

- Critical thinking: The ability to look at problems in a critical manner that allows for new thinking and solving problems across multiple subjects and disciplines.

- Communication: The ability to share and exchange thoughts and ideas, ask questions, and discuss solutions to problems.

- Collaboration: The ability to work together for a mutual goal or outcome using one's talent, expertise, and knowledge.

- Creativity: The ability to think of new ideas and approaches in an innovative and inventive manner.

As responsive caregivers, we want to prepare children for the future. We want to build on children's natural curiosity and desire to explore as we encourage the development of the Four Cs. When you learn to recognize the Four Cs, you'll see that they are already present in what you do each day to assist children in their learning. Some everyday examples of how the Four Cs can be found in an infant-toddler learning environment are shown on page 20.

High-quality programs plan activities that promote critical thinking, communication, collaboration, and creativity along with promoting STEM education. Play-based activities are the perfect vehicle for introducing the Four Cs. You will see throughout the STEM activities in this book how each of the Four Cs are embedded in the activities and in the inquiry questions you ask young children. I believe that infant-toddler STEM is present in the everyday activities provided in high-quality learning environments; however, you might be thinking, "Is it too premature to address these skills when working with infants and toddlers?" "Where do developmentally appropriate practices and play factor into this STEM movement?" These are great questions, and I'm glad you're thinking about them! As we intentionally care for children, we need to consider the role of developmentally appropriate practice (DAP) and play in the early learning environment. As responsive caregivers, we understand that children learn best in DAP environments.

EXAMPLES OF THE FOUR Cs IN ACTION

Four Cs	Teacher inter-actions and open-ended questions	Infants	Toddlers	Twos
Critical thinking	The caregiver models to a baby how to place plastic shapes into a sorting bucket. Caregiver asks children what, why, and how questions to promote their critical thinking skills.	An infant places plastic shapes in a sorting bucket without assistance. Later she takes the top off the bucket and repeats the activity using additional objects, testing to see if they will fit inside the bucket.	A child practices trial and error as he scoops sand and fills a bucket and pours it out, then repeats the process. A child fills a sieve with sand and watches it fall through.	A child begins to put puzzles together, manipulating pieces in the correct place in order to complete the puzzle.
Communication	The caregiver demonstrates language structure by exhibiting self-talk. For example, "I'm going to lift the top of this box so we can put the toy inside."	A baby raises her arms, communicating that she wants to be picked up by the caregiver.	A toddler carrying a book walks over to a caregiver, smiles, and says, "Book read."	A two-year-old communicates to the caregiver that he wants to ride the tricycle. He says, "I need your help," communicating that he needs help putting on the safety helmet.
Collaboration	Caregiver sets up activities that allow for collaboration. Caregiver exhibits self-talk by saying, "I see my friend Andy playing next to Megan at the water table." She asks the children to share about their play, saying, "What does the water feel like?"	A baby observes another baby playing beside her.	A toddler begins parallel play, sharing the toy cars with another child.	A two-year-old engages in sensory play with another child and shares his toy cars. The child waits his turn to play and says, "Here's a car for you."
Creativity	Caregiver observes children playing and introduces new play materials to expand their creativity.	A baby shakes a rattle and then taps it against the floor to explore how it sounds.	A toddler makes the sound "vroom vroom" to imitate the sound of a car.	A two-year-old engages in dress-up, pretending to be a fire fighter, and uses a foam noodle to put out a pretend fire.

EARLY LEARNING ENVIRONMENTS

In high-quality early learning environments, caring adults provide infants and toddlers with a variety of learning experiences in a safe, clean, and supportive space where young children are encouraged to play and explore. Infants and toddlers need responsive caregivers who provide engaging materials that are developmentally appropriate for young children. (Specific materials will be discussed later in the book.) Best practices in early childhood state that children develop and learn best in environments designed for their chronological and developmental age. According to Carol Copple and Sue Bredekamp (2009), DAP include the following concepts:

- Teachers meet children at their individual level of development.

- Teachers use strategies that are appropriate to the child's age and developmental status.

- Teachers recognize the unique capabilities of each child.

- Environments are responsive to the social and cultural factors of the child.

- Environments promote progress and interest among children.

DAP is a common term in the field of child development. It is an early childhood perspective whereby a caregiver nurtures a child's social-emotional, physical, and cognitive growth. Through an integrated approach, DAP environments are perfect places to introduce and teach the principles and practices of STEM. They are designed so both indoor and outdoor spaces and activities are age appropriate and accessible for all children, including children with special needs and disabilities. Developmentally appropriate settings allow children time to learn new skills and practice competencies previously mastered. They provide learning experiences that enhance children's skills across developmental domains. Early learning environments that use DAP approaches enhance the STEM learning opportunities for infants and toddlers.

Beginning from birth, high-quality learning environments nurture the whole child. Responsive caregivers provide a variety of activities and materials so children can freely explore their environment. Children are naturally curious and love to explore, which makes the selection of educational materials in your learning environment very important. Educational materials and toys for young children are objects for exploration that enhance or stimulate a child's learning. As you examine your early learning environment, review the checklist below to see if you have age-appropriate STEM materials in your classroom.

✓ My classroom has a variety of tools such as magnifying glasses, tongs, eyedroppers, scale or balance, and magnets that children can use for investigation.

✓ My classroom has a variety of books about farm life, the ocean, the forest, life cycle of bugs and insects, and the zoo.

✓ My classroom has blocks and recyclable materials for building and engineering.

✓ My classroom has manipulatives and objects for counting and sorting.

✓ My classroom has balls and sensory materials.

✔ My classroom has cars, trucks, and wheeled toys for pushing and pulling.

✔ My classroom has living things that grow and change over time.

✔ My classroom has objects that reflect light and shadows.

✔ My classroom has outdoor materials for sand and sensory play.

Developmentally appropriate learning environments and intentional planning provide children with opportunities to explore and expand their STEM learning. Responsive caregivers are intentional in their interactions with young children. Intentional teaching is recognized as a best teaching practice for all children. Intentional teachers plan activities and dialogue with children with specific outcomes and goals in mind (Epstein 2007). They have a deep understanding of the ages and stages of the children in their care. Intentional teachers adapt the learning environment and activities to meet the changing developmental needs of each child, thus allowing children to maximize their learning opportunities. The following are characteristics of intentional early learning environments:

- High expectations: Teachers assume children are capable of reaching reasonable educational goals and engage children in ways that will assist them in reaching these expectations.

- Planning and management: Teachers spend time planning intentional age-appropriate activities designed to help children connect new learning to prior learning. Teachers reflect on their teaching strategies and planning. Teachers manage both individual and group dynamics in ways that promote children's interests.

- Learning-oriented classroom: Teachers recognize the early environment is a place for learning.

- Engaging activities: Teachers plan activities that reflect the developmental stage for each child. They are sensitive to planning activities that don't overestimate or underestimate the child's developmental age and ability.

- Thoughtful questioning: Teachers plan and actively engage children's thinking and promote natural curiosity through thoughtful questions and prompts.

- Feedback: Teachers support children's natural curiosity and desire to construct knowledge through positive feedback.

Intentional caregivers create a balance between child-directed and adult-directed experiences. In child-directed learning, children explore freely with adult guidance, allowing them to construct their own meaning from the play experience. In adult-directed experiences, teachers design and set up the environment, introducing information, modeling skills, demonstrating how to use tools, and promoting concept understanding through dialogue and open-ended questions (Epstein 2007). For example, a caregiver plans an outdoor water play activity focusing on evaporation. Here the teacher plans for the children to use large paintbrushes to "paint" the sidewalk. She begins by modeling the activity and introduces the basic principle of evaporation. She will share with the children that water can take on different forms: liquid, solid, and gas. She will state that there is water in the bucket and also on the paintbrush. "Let's feel the water. The water is liquid. What happens when we brush the water on the sidewalk? That's right, the water changes and makes it look wet. What's happening now? Look, the water is disappearing. That's called evaporation!" (See Look What Absorbs! activity, page 110.) Responsive caregivers understand children need the freedom to explore and play; with intentional planning, we can help promote and scaffold learning across the developmental domains.

Developmentally appropriate STEM activities should be integrated throughout the learning environment. Caregivers who plan meaningful activities allow children to move forward on the developmental continuum without overly taxing them. Responsive caregivers understand that young children need time to play and explore. The late infant education expert Magna Gerber, founder of the Resources for Infant Educares (aka The RIE Method), strongly advocated for caregivers to allow children time to play and explore. She felt that caregivers should allow young children opportunities to explore the world around them at their own pace. The RIE philosophy advocates for caregivers to have respect for and trust in the baby to be an initiator, explorer, and self-learner (Gerber and Sunbury 2012). As you plan

STEM activities and select materials for play, consider each child's developmental needs and allow them time for exploration.

Well-planned, intentional activities build on children's natural interest and curiosity. In developmentally appropriate early care, caregivers speak to children respectfully, listen carefully, and promote critical thinking and integrative learning. These are the building blocks of the Four Cs that we addressed earlier. In developmentally appropriate learning environments, caregivers understand the importance of nurturing the whole child and provide opportunities for children to grow and develop across the learning domains. Caregivers and parents partner to support each other and communicate openly on ways to support the child's learning across the curriculum. In developmentally appropriate early care centers, parents are engaged in their children's learning. Parents and caregivers work collaboratively to support the home-school connection.

In developmentally appropriate early care centers, caregivers respond to the individual needs of each child through intentional play-based activities. Throughout this book, you will notice that the STEM experiences designed for use in our early learning settings are always play based and incorporate DAP. This is intentional because developmentally appropriate practices and children's play work in unison to provide optimal learning for young children. Activities that are developmentally appropriate and intentionally designed help meet the social-emotional, physical, and cognitive growth of young children. Play offers children opportunities to build on children's growing skills and prior learning. Play provides a context for children to organize their thinking. Play-based activities engage children's natural sense of wonder and exploration as they learn about the world.

Educational Materials and Toys

Early learning environments should provide infants and toddlers with a variety of educational materials and toys in both indoor and outdoor areas. Infant-toddler materials should be developmentally appropriate and offer ways for the child to actively engage in the learning process. STEM materials need to be easily manipulated by infants and toddlers. Babies and young children need time to taste, handle, and manipulate new objects. Don't rush them or interrupt their learning process. Many times caregivers stop children in the middle of their play and exploration to ask questions such as "What are you building?" or "Can you tell me what you're doing?" Asking questions when children are in the midst of their play interrupts their thinking and learning process. My suggestion is to sit or stand near the child. When the child looks up or *naturally* stops playing, ask questions and engage in a conversation. Think of how you might feel if you were working on something intently and someone were to interrupt your concentration with questions. Asking questions is an important part of the learning process. But take your time and only ask questions when the child

is ready. Watch and observe the cues. Engage in dialogue with the child and be sure to document what you see. Child-directed learning is important. Giving infants and toddlers plenty of opportunities to explore freely allows them to direct and construct their own learning.

Responsive caregivers know children need time and space for exploration. Through careful observation, we know that children explore their play materials at their own pace. Babies will mouth and manipulate an object before moving on to something new. Remember that the brain seeks novelty. Provide new and interesting objects for the child to investigate and discover. We often see a child come back to an interesting object again and again. It's as if they want to learn more and more about it! Responsive caregivers provide lots of open-ended play experiences for children as they investigate and explore their environment.

Open-ended play is important for self-discovery and learning. I've found that caregivers often move children from one activity to another before the child has finished playing. Keeping to a schedule is important, but young children need plenty of unstructured time for exploration and discovery. Magda Gerber once said that those working with infants and toddlers should "Go slowly with great patience" (Gerber 2016). She felt that

infants needed opportunities and time to take in and figure out the world around them. When planning materials for STEM learning, caregivers should consider the interests and attention span of infants and toddlers. Responsive caregivers select materials that also scaffold the child's learning, building on prior knowledge and skills.

Materials should be selected with intention. Ask yourself the following questions: How will the child use this toy to learn? What does this toy teach the child? How can I scaffold the child's learning and help him make connections to prior knowledge? For example, how you organize children's toys is important. Toys should be positioned and organized so children can access them easily. Low storage shelves can be used to store items and to help stabilize children who are learning to walk. Things that are different shapes and colors add interest for the child. It's also important not to have too many toys and objects out at one time. More is not always the best approach with young children. Selecting safe educational materials, including toys and objects, is an important component of a high-quality program.

Safety

Safety must always be considered when selecting toys and planning activities. When purchasing items, such as rattles and small toys, always read the manufacturer's label to ensure the play materials are age appropriate and meet United States Consumer Product Safety Commission guidelines. Toys for children birth to age three should be durable, easy to clean, and large enough that pieces cannot be swallowed or cause choking. Since children who are younger than three years of age primarily explore with their senses, they tend to put everything in their mouths. This puts infants and toddlers at a high risk for swallowing objects and choking. When choosing items for the activities in this book, be careful in your selection. Always consider safety first. Infants and toddlers should be closely supervised to make sure they don't place small objects in their mouth. There are baby care devices that enable adults to check the size of an

object to determine if it is too small for an infant or toddler to play with and poses a choking hazard to young children. Never let young children play with small items, such as marbles, small balls, or objects with small pieces that could be a choking hazard. Avoid toys with sharp edges and points and toys that might leak or break apart when mouthed or bitten into by a young child. Young children pull, squeeze, and twist toys; therefore, toys should be checked frequently for safety and breakage.

It is important to verify that products have been tested carefully, are nontoxic, and are age appropriate. Stuffed animals and dolls should have hair, buttons, and accessories sewn securely in place. Remove stuffed animals and dolls that have items glued or stapled to them and always remove paper tags. The activities in this book use crayons, markers, chalk, paint, and other creative art materials. Be sure you use materials labeled nontoxic. The Art and Creative Materials Institute identifies art, craft, and creative materials that are nontoxic and safe for children. It is recommended that these classroom art materials have their Approved Product (AP) seal of approval. For more information about the products bearing the AP seal of approval go to www.acminet.org.

Choose toys that are made of thick, durable, heavy plastic or solid wood. Solid wood, including building blocks, should be smooth and have no rough or splintery edges. Plastic items should be free of the toxic chemical bisphenol A (BPA) and be labeled BPA-free. To minimize the risk of purchasing lead-contaminated or toxic products, purchase items that meet the United States Consumer Product Safety Commission Standards. The United States Consumer Product Safety Commission also lists toys that have been recalled. For more information on toy safety go to www.cpsc .gov/business–manufacturing/business-education /toy-safety or to the Toy Industry Association at www.toyassociation.org.

Adults must check the materials frequently to make sure they are in good repair and dispose of any items that are broken, chipped, or can pose a danger to young children. Children's toys should be cleaned and disinfected regularly according to the center's policies. Avoid toys and objects with strings or cords, which can be dangerous for infants and toddlers. Children can drown in just a few inches of water; therefore, any activity that includes water play should always be closely supervised. The safety and well-being of a young child is the responsibility of all caregivers. Infants and toddlers should be well supervised at all times.

STEM Early Learning Centers

When planning STEM activities and materials for learning centers, I suggest that caregivers consider focusing on one or two learning principles at a time. For example, one week you might focus on balls, motion, and gravity. For this unit, start with several different-sized balls for the children to use in play. After a few days, introduce new balls that have different textures and make different sounds. The focus of this learning is that balls come in different sizes, have different textures, and can be rolled and shaken. Expand infants' learning by introducing motion and gravity to the play with the use of inclined planes. Model how to roll a ball down a ramp and say, "Tonya has the ball in her hand. As she lets it go, it rolls down the ramp. See how fast it goes." Learning centers help young children begin to group and classify STEM concepts together. Well-organized centers are not just helpful to you as a caregiver but are beneficial to the children's learning. Children will learn where certain play materials belong in the center. They learn the math concepts of how to sort materials and classify materials. For example, all the rocks go in this basket and all the plastic shapes go in another. The big balls stay outdoors. These early steps of sorting and categorizing begin to introduce young children to concepts of math. Here are some suggestions for organizing STEM centers in your early learning environment and the materials that support STEM learning:

The following is a list of materials that support STEM learning in an infant-toddler classroom:

- soft foam blocks
- cardboard blocks
- paint
- paintbrushes
- buckets
- watering can
- crayons
- paper
- scissors
- washable markers
- colored chalk
- measuring cups
- measuring spoons
- plastic trays

- newsprint
- clean coffee filters in various sizes
- straws
- strawberry cartons
- egg cartons
- string
- yarn

- paper bags
- plastic bottles
- wooden clothespins
- nature center pamphlets
- instruments, such as maracas, drums, and rhythm sticks

Best practices state that STEM learning occurs in all areas of the learning environment. Therefore, STEM learning materials should be placed throughout the learning environment. STEM learning should not be limited to the science center or block area only, but incorporated throughout the center. Children should have easy access to STEM materials for both indoor and outdoor explorations. Select STEM materials that are simple and can be used by young children with little frustration. When organizing materials for the classroom, try to select storage materials made out of wood or natural fibers. Again, remember that the developing brain seeks novelty. Add new materials to extend the learning and exploration of the child.

- plastic bowls
- plastic cups
- plastic and wooden spoons
- magnifying glass
- magnets
- magnet wands
- hand lenses
- prisms
- eyedroppers
- classroom scale
- classroom balance scale

- books
- camera
- balls of different sizes, weights, and textures
- cars
- trucks
- light table
- sand and sand toys
- water table and water toys
- play fruits and vegetables
- play animals

And here are materials that can be repurposed for classroom use. Make sure that all items are clean and don't have small loose parts or sharp edges.

- cardboard tubing from paper towels or wrapping paper

- cardboard boxes
- small wood blocks

Early learning centers	STEM	Suggested materials
Things that roll and bounce	Science Math	Balls of various sizes
Things that fit inside another object	Engineering Math	Small- to medium-size storage containers and small objects that can be placed inside the containers. For example, a small colored cotton scarf that can fit inside a plastic storage container
Things that go on top or can be stacked	Science Engineering Math	Commercially purchased stackable toys, soft building blocks, and small containers that allow objects to be stacked on top
Things that are smooth and rough	Science	Balls with different textures, sandpaper blocks, wood blocks, rubber ducks, different textured fabrics
Things that are shiny or sticky	Science	A variety of shiny objects, including bells, kitchen utensils, and mirrors. A paper ball made from duct tape, with the sticky side on the outside
Things that reflect light and can be seen through	Science Technology	A variety of different-sized mirrors, color paddles, magnetic tile shapes such as Magna-Tiles; play materials that are clear and see-through; magnifying glass for older children
Things that can be pounded or pushed	Science Technology Math	A variety of items that can be pounded with a hammer or pushed into holes. Pounding tools and pegboards
Things that are alike but come in different sizes	Science Math	Similar objects in different sizes, such as toy cows, horses, and pigs, or shapes in different sizes and colors that can be counted and sorted
Things with wheels	Science	A variety of cars, trucks, wood animal toys with wheels, wagons, shopping carts, wheeled toys that stabilize new walkers
Things that open and shut	Science Technology	A variety of toys with doors or latches that can be opened and shut
Things that make noise when you shake or squeeze them	Science	Different types of rattles, sensory balls, and sensory bottles (See activities Liquid Sensory Bottles, page 108; Rattle and Shake Sensory Bottle, page 130; and Ribbon Shakers, page 132.)
Things that can be used for scooping, grasping, and building	Technology Engineering	Ice cream scoops, tongs, large plastic tweezers, shovels, wooden spoons, soft building blocks, and plastic containers
Things that have wings	Science	A variety of toy butterflies, bees, birds. Seeing living things with wings is great too.
Things that hop	Science	A variety of toy rabbits, frogs, grasshoppers, and kangaroos. Seeing living things that hop is great too.

DOCUMENTATION: CAPTURING LEARNING MOMENTS

High-quality early learning environments recognize the importance of documenting children's learning. Infants and toddlers are constantly on the go; therefore it's important to capture these learning moments quickly. Understanding different strategies of documentation is essential to quality care and STEM education. Each activity in this book will provide you with opportunities to document children's STEM learning. Through documentation, caregivers carefully observe and collect children's work, take photographs of them playing and learning, record audio or video of play experiences, and/or take anecdotal records. Each form of documentation provides adults with opportunities to tell the story of the learning process and the purpose of an event, experience, or development taking place in their early learning environment (Seitz 2008). Caregivers analyze and interpret their documentation in order to measure children's learning on the developmental continuum and for future planning. Responsive caregivers use this information as they plan intentional activities to scaffold and introduce new learning.

Early care providers use documentation strategies throughout their day in order to capture children's exploration, discovery, and learning. Caregivers use what they learn through observation and documentation to plan and organize intentional early learning opportunities. In play experiences, responsive caregivers are actively engaged in supporting children's learning. They need to describe the activity to the children, introduce the STEM concepts, provide prompts, ask open-ended questions, and teach new vocabulary words. Each interaction and engagement helps children connect new knowledge to prior learning. Engaging in conversations with young children and modeling language and vocabulary is incorporated into each of the STEM learning activities. Each activity in this book has a list of vocabulary words, questions to ask, and things to say to support the learning process. Use these tools to support classroom documentation and to deepen the STEM learning experience. Documentations may include scribing what children say and think about an activity. For example, you might document children painting with water outside. In this STEM opportunity, the children paint with water and then observe the process of evaporation. The caregiver would invite the children to share their thoughts and feelings about the water play activity. For example, a child might describe the experience by saying, "It was wet." Another child might say, "It's gone! It disappeared." Asking inquiry questions such as "What does the sidewalk look like when we paint it?" or "What do you think happened to the water?" allows the caregiver opportunities to assess the child's thinking and understanding of the water play activity. Additionally, the caregiver can assess the child's developing language skills while promoting vocabulary development. In each of the STEM activities, you will have opportunities to document children's learning. It is important to make documentation an integral part of responsive caregiving.

One strategy for documentation is the use of photographs and video recordings. How often do we think, "Oh, I should document that!" or "Wait a minute, let me get my camera!" before the moment is gone? It's true, a picture is worth a thousand words. A photo captures the child's

expression and sense of wonder. Photos can tell a story and help parents and observers see the purpose of the play experience. A photo or video can capture what interests a child, her facial expressions, and powerful moments of new individual learning. When taking documentation photos, you will have the best results when you move to the children's level so you can capture what they see from their vantage point. It's not important that the children look at the camera for documentation; your job is to capture the moments of learning and discovery. If possible, caregivers should take daily photographs of children exploring or investigating STEM activities.

Posting photographs throughout the classroom is another great strategy for infant-toddler caregivers. Post photographs of an event or ongoing children's STEM play experiences on a bulletin board. One place to hang a bulletin board is near the parent sign-in area. Change the photos each week or every other week to show parents and children what activities and learning have taken place. Also place bulletin boards at eye level in several areas of the early learning environment so children can see themselves engaging in the play. Placing photos in clear acrylic picture frames allows children to see their learning too. Arranging photos throughout the early learning environment provides a place for teachers and children to revisit the activity and reinforce the learning and STEM concept words taught. And children love to see pictures of themselves!

Documentation should provide evidence to parents that learning is a process and that children's engagement through play is essential. Here the use of technology provides caregivers with a way to document children's learning. A computer is another useful way of displaying children's work. Run photos as a slide show on a computer where parents arrive to pick up children at the end of the day. Have the computer play the slide show continuously so parents and children alike can see the fun and learning that goes on during the day. If you have permission to share or post photos on the center's website, that's another way for parents to see what their children are doing. This is especially useful for grandparents and other family members who live far away! Photos displaying what children did during the day provide parents with an opportunity to stay connected to their children and tuned in to the early learning experience.

Portfolios are another form of documentation that support the learning process of infants and toddlers. Collecting evidence of developmental progress helps caregivers measure children's growth along the developmental continuum. Keep a running record of anecdotal notes on each child. Place the anecdotal records in your portfolio where you describe what you see and hear children doing. Try to be as factual as possible. Provide enough detail to enable you to use this information as part of the assessment process. In the portfolio, caregivers also place samples of children's work, providing a means to evaluate how children are growing and mastering skills over time. In the following scenario, the children have planted a garden, as they learn about earth and life science. The caregiver might ask a three-year-old to draw a picture of the garden. She would document the young child's drawing at the beginning, middle, and end of the year. To assess a child's developmental growth, the caregiver would then compare each of the child's drawings to previous drawing samples. The caregiver might see random scribbling on the first documentation, more controlled scribbling mid-year, and more lines and patterns appearing in drawings at the end of the year. An older three-year-old might demonstrate evidence of lines, patterns, and curves looking more like letters or objects. In this example, the caregiver is connecting the STEM earth and life science activity to a developmental assessment. When children complete work, it is collected and then added to their portfolio. Of course, some of the work is sent home or displayed in the classroom too! Each sample represents the progress, or lack of progress, a child is making across the developmental continuum. Effective documentation provides evidence or a snapshot of where they are on the developmental continuum in different learning domains.

Documentation is a useful tool for evaluating children's developmental growth over time. A teacher might say to a parent, "I think Carlos is doing better." This statement sounds positive and encouraging to parents, but it's not enough. In quality infant-toddler care, caregivers need evidence documenting a child's developmental status in order to initiate an intentional and meaningful conversation. A portfolio of Carlos's work documents his growth over time. For example, to examine his cognitive and reasoning skills, the caregiver needs to demonstrate concrete evidence of his current developmental status. Through transcribing what Carlos experiences in a STEM activity, a caregiver could document Carlos's thinking, reasoning, and expressive language skills. A collection of his artwork would show his fine-motor skills. A photograph of Carlos exploring the growing vegetables in the garden will demonstrate his curiosity and interest in new things.

Careful documentation provides caregivers with concrete evidence to share with parents. Together parents and teachers can partner to support the child's growth and development. Solid documentation and intentional conversations allow parents and caregivers opportunities to work together to support the child's growth and development. Documenting children's growth and development provides caregivers with the evidence needed to modify and adapt the learning environment to meet the developmental needs of all children. If there are any developmental delay concerns, documentation will be useful when referrals for interventions are being considered.

3

Enhancing STEM Learning in Young Children

The foundation of STEM learning is based on both children's natural interest and innate desire to learn about the world and the introduction of STEM principles through intentional planning by educators. Responsive caregivers plan developmentally appropriate play-based STEM activities that build on children's natural curiosity and sense of wonder. Children birth through age two are constantly learning about the world through exploration. Each new experience and exploration provides children with new learning opportunities. Children learn about STEM through their five senses and hands-on experiences. Early educators build STEM learning through reading and talking with children and capitalizing on teachable moments. Responsive caregivers understand the integrated nature of STEM learning. As children learn about science, for example, they might also be exposed to or experience elements of technology and mathematics. Refer to the activity index on page 177 to see how activities incorporate various aspects of STEM. For example, the Build a Bridge activity focuses on Science, Technology, Engineering, and Mathematics while the Ribbon Shakers activity focuses on Science and Technology. As responsive caregivers plan and integrate STEM learning into the early learning environment, they will see that scientific inquiry is embedded into children's learning and is a key element in STEM education.

SCIENTIFIC INQUIRY

The foundation of STEM in the early years is based on children's interest in scientific inquiry. Scientific inquiry sparks children's natural curiosity about the world. We spoke earlier about children being called "little scientists." Responsive caregivers play an integral role in helping children deepen their understanding of STEM. Responsive caregivers build and enhance children's learning by responding to children's natural curiosity and

desire for exploration. They design developmentally appropriate activities and engage in playful interactions, all of which promote children's natural desire to learn. Multiple learning opportunities for exploration and discovery set the stage for children to construct scientific knowledge. Responsive caregivers promote scientific inquiry in young children by listening and observing, asking questions, paraphrasing, and prompting extended learning.

Listening and Observing Children

In high-quality early care, adults listen and observe children carefully. Caregivers attend to the verbal and nonverbal cues from children. Babies communicate their interests through gestures such as kicking their feet or hands in excitement, smiling, gurgling, and squealing. Toddlers will show interest in objects and inquiry as they manipulate and investigate materials. As children get older, they will engage caregivers in their play and exploration while asking How, What, and Why questions. As children's cognitions develop, so do their language skills and their ability to communicate. Asking and answering children's questions is an essential part of STEM learning in infant-toddler care.

Asking Questions

In a high-quality early learning environment, children are encouraged to ask questions. Caregivers respond thoughtfully, respectfully, and in a timely manner to children's questions. No question is too small or insignificant to a responsive caregiver. Responsive caregivers encourage children's questions and understand that they have a deep-rooted need to learn about the world and how it works. Remember that during these early years, children are building schemas and formulating theories, gaining knowledge that is the foundation for future learning. Caregivers also ask open-ended questions and provide prompts to expand children's cognitive development. Inquiry questions help stimulate thinking and

problem-solving skills in children. They provide opportunities for children to develop and expand vocabulary and language skills.

Open-ended questions are a key component of scientific inquiry. Inquiry questions help children or "little scientists" investigate and explore possibilities. Inquiry questions include the following:

- Why?

- When?

- Where?

- What?

- How?

Here are some suggestions on how to use open-ended questions to promote children's learning.

Use What and When questions to

- enhance children's observation skills;

- clarify children's thinking;

- focus current play;

- build vocabulary;

- draw inferences and conclusions.

Use Why, Where, and How questions to

- build reasoning skills;
- deepen content knowledge;
- further exploration;
- build on previous learning;
- make predictions;
- measure and classify.

Use prompts and comments to

- connect prior learning.

Another good teaching practice that supports both language development and inquiry skills is to paraphrase what children say and the questions they ask. In paraphrasing, the adult restates what the child says or asks and then adds clarifying comments on additional vocabulary words, or states ways to extend the child's thinking. This also provides the caregiver with an opportunity to model correct grammar and sentence structure. For example, a child points and says, "See car go." You might paraphrase or restate what the child said by saying, "I see it go. I see the car *rolling* down the ramp. It's *moving* fast." For an older toddler, you might expand the discussion and learning by saying, "*Gravity* is causing the car to roll down the ramp. What else could we use to roll down the ramp?" Paraphrasing provides opportunities for the child to gain knowledge and understanding in a supportive way while expanding their inquiry skills.

Scientific inquiry is essential to quality infant-toddler care. Through listening, observing, and asking questions, children and caregivers deepen their relationship. Children's inquiry stimulates other children's thinking and inquiry too. Creating an environment that promotes scientific inquiry also promotes the Four Cs. Whether it's building with blocks, playing at a sensory table, or playing with cars or balls, children of all ages are learning about STEM using the scientific method. Now that we know the importance of play and responsive caregiving, let's look specifically at the components of STEM.

INTRODUCTION TO SCIENCE

Young children have a sense of wonder about science. Science is observing, investigating, and exploring the world. Whether playing in the sand, mixing paint colors, planting seeds in the soil, or investigating bugs and insects, young children have a natural interest in the world around them. They love to explore materials and play with objects, such as building blocks, balls, and cars. They are intrigued with bugs and insects. They are eager to learn and discover more and more about science. It's important to remember that science is everywhere. The principles of science relate to everything around us. It's the air we breathe, the water we drink, and the food we eat. Science might seem like something complicated and technical, but in reality science is fairly simple. My guess is that you're probably doing a lot of science already as you work with young children. Do you take babies on walks outside and point out the trees and the flowers you see? Do you invite them to listen and observe the birds in the trees? Do you sit on the floor and roll a ball back and forth with a child? Do you offer children different things to smell and taste, such as different kinds of fruits? As they play in a sandbox or at a water table, do you think about what other materials you could add to help them learn about the properties of sand and water? If you answered yes to any or all of these questions, you're already on your way to teaching science to your infants and toddlers. Many people think that science is hard to understand, complicated, and sometimes a little mysterious. In truth, the basics of science are quite straightforward. The truth is science is everywhere, and children experience it through everyday activities.

Science is a way of organizing, recording, and testing what we know and think about the world. You don't have to have an extensive knowledge about science to introduce the principles of it to young children. I encourage you to be excited and engaged with the children as they explore and discover their world. I think half the fun of caring for infants, toddlers, and twos is learning and playing with them. No one expects you to know it all. Just join in the fun and become a "co-explorer" with them. When introducing STEM to young children you will see that science plays a key role in all other forms of STEM. It would be rare to not find some element of science in all play experiences. Remember, we are building the foundation for future STEM learning. Here is a list of science vocabulary words you might consider as you build a foundation of STEM for young children:

Understanding basic science vocabulary will help as you build and scaffold children's understanding of science. The vocabulary can be a refresher for you too as you deepen your understanding of the principles and concepts of science along with the children.

Often educators think of science as one concentration but in truth science is composed of different concentrations: physical science, life science, and earth science. Each concentration examines science within its own paradigm. Physical, life, and earth sciences are each unique in their makeup and characteristics. These three branches of science present areas of expertise and research. For example, physicists explore the properties of matter and energy and the relationship between them; biologists answer questions about the study of living things; and geologists study rocks and the earth. All areas of science incorporate observation and investigation and answer specific scientific questions. Regardless of the different branches of science, the fundamentals of science all build on inquiry and exploration.

Physical Science

Physical science is everywhere, and children are learning about it every day. Physical science studies the characteristics and physical properties of nonliving objects, including solid and liquid materials, and how those objects and materials change. Physical science explores changes

- absorption
- buoyancy
- bouncy
- build
- cause and effect
- design
- engineer
- experiment
- flexibility
- force
- freeze
- frozen
- gravity
- habitat
- height
- inclined plane
- investigate
- inquiry
- length
- liquid
- matter
- melt
- motion
- observation
- shape
- size
- solid
- tool
- temperature
- texture

and transformations in objects and materials and the motion of objects. Does this sound too advanced for infants and toddlers? Let me break it down into everyday learning. Physical science in the care setting focuses on children's ability to explore and describe properties of objects such as size, shape, weight, texture, and flexibility. As I shared earlier, introducing STEM in infant-toddler classrooms is done informally through play-based activities.

Physical science is embedded into our developmentally appropriate activities and play experiences. When children are building with blocks they are learning physical properties of height, weight, stability, and gravity. As they pick up different-sized blocks for play, they observe that some blocks are smaller and weigh less than others. Older children may play with blocks made of different materials, and each block may weigh and feel different than other wood blocks. At a water table, children learn about weight, density, and buoyancy during a sink and float activity. In play experiences, children learn about cause and effect and that materials can change to look and feel different. For example, when children mix two or three colors of paint together, new colors appear. Children learn about force and gravity as they roll, bounce, and throw balls. The activities

in this book offer many opportunities to introduce young children to the principles, concepts, and vocabulary of science. Here are lists of activities and materials that can be used to introduce children birth to two years to science.

Infants

- watching a mobile move
- playing with sensory balls
- shaking rattles that make different sounds
- pushing buttons on toys that light up or make noise
- going for walks outside
- sitting outside
- smelling scents
- watching objects move in the wind
- feeling the wind on their faces
- watching a ball roll and bounce
- feeling water on their hands
- kicking or swatting objects while on their backs
- reading board books with pictures of nature and science content

Toddlers

- stacking objects
- building and exploring cardboard or foam building blocks
- filling objects with water and then pouring it out
- rolling balls back and forth with a caregiver
- bouncing balls
- climbing up a play structure
- sliding down a play structure
- beating a drum and feeling the vibrations
- playing with realistic plastic animals

- playing with realistic plastic fruits and vegetables

- reading books with nature and science content

- playing with sand toys, such as large spoons, shovels, buckets, sieves, measuring cups, and funnels

- playing with cars and balls on simple ramps and pathways

- playing with water play toys, such as buckets, measuring cups, spoons, pitchers, and water wheels

Twos

- playing with wood puzzles of numbers, shapes, and natural objects

- building and exploring with cardboard or soft blocks

- playing with realistic plastic animals

- playing with realistic plastic fruits and vegetables

- playing in kitchen and dramatic play areas

- bouncing and catching a ball

- rolling a ball down an incline and running and picking it up

- using large magnet wands

- using large, sturdy magnifying glasses

- creating and exploring sensory bottles

- reading books with nature and science content

- playing with cars and trucks

- building complex ramps and pathways for cars and balls

- building complex bridges and block structures (using imaginative play)

- playing with manipulatives for counting and sorting

It's easy to see that science is present in the everyday activities of our early learning environment. Reading books such as *Big Board First 100 Machines, Little Blue Truck, Tap Tap Bang Bang,* and *Toot Toot Beep Beep* provides opportunities for children to connect experiences with literature. The more intentional a caregiver is in planning and engaging children in the STEM learning process, the richer the experience is for young children.

Life Science

Life science examines the properties and characteristics of living things. It includes understanding and appreciating how living things, such as plants and animals, grow and change over time. Exploration of life science allows children to closely observe the physical characteristics, behaviors, habitats, and needs of living things. Learning about life science includes understanding our bodies and how we, as humans, grow and change over time. In life science, children learn that there is diversity and variations in all living things. Responsive caregivers plan intentional experiences where children can sort, classify, and look for patterns in living things. For example, a class might go for a walk to collect leaves and later investigate the differences and similarities between leaves they collected. Caregivers ask inquiry questions as they engage children in conversations about what they observe. They introduce new vocabulary words, helping children connect real-life objects and experiences to new words. Responsive caregivers intentionally plan activities to provide young children with opportunities to investigate and explore the natural world.

In an early learning environment, caregivers intentionally plan for life science experiences. It might be simply planting seeds and watching them grow. Here you would want to document the process of planting the seeds and watching the seeds change over time. It's recommended that caregivers read books about the characteristics of animals, what sounds they make, their physical appearance, and the habitats where they live. They provide pictures of living things for children to examine. It is best to use real pictures or realia rather than drawings. Bring living things and real objects into your early learning environment. This might be a plant, fish tank, or class pet. Living things in your classroom provide children with opportunities to see how they grow and change, and learn how to care for them. Observing and caring for pets deepens children's understanding of life science. Having living things in your classroom helps children learn respect and care for living things. It provides caregivers with many teachable moments.

Teachable moments offer caregivers opportunities to extend children's learning. For example, if you are outside and a child sees a caterpillar crawling on the grass, you have an opportunity to teach more about the life cycle of a butterfly. Nature provides endless opportunities to introduce life science to young children. Point out things you see in the sky, such as clouds or birds flying. Invite children to look at the leaves on a tree moving or the snow or rain falling. Each interaction is an opportunity to teach. Watch and observe children carefully. You'll see their natural curiosity and inquiry when they explore nature. It might be the smallest bug or a bird landing on a branch. Each spark of interest offers you a teachable moment. Take the time to deepen children's learning during these precious moments of inquiry. Children will capture your excitement about living things. Share your enthusiasm about living things with them. Teachable moments express to children that learning is everywhere. With your active engagement as a care provider, every moment is a teachable moment. Think of the outdoors as part of the classroom curriculum where children are free to explore and discover nature.

Caregivers build on prior learning through intentional thematic curriculum. Again, when teaching STEM you start with the basics and build on children's prior knowledge. You might focus on a theme of farm animals where you intentionally focus on the animals that live on a farm. Here you would talk about cows, horses, pigs, ducks,

and chickens. You might read the book and sing the song "Old Macdonald Had a Farm." Remember that we want to read both fiction and nonfiction books to young children. Other suggestions for life science books include *The Grouchy Ladybug*, *Where Butterflies Grow*, *Tacky the Penguin*, and *The Bugliest Bug*. Children need to engage in the fun of storytelling as well as learn factual information. Other life science themes that would be developmentally appropriate for this age group would be the ocean, bugs and insects, the forest, and jungle animals. Establishing themes helps children organize their new thinking and learning around common features. The vocabulary they learn around a theme helps them in classifying objects. Thematic units do not necessarily need to be formal or from a publisher, they just need to be well planned, have intentional teaching, be play based, and include hands-on activities.

Active engagement with nature and living things is a large part of STEM learning. Young children learn about nature through hands-on experiences. Spend lots of time outdoors, letting children naturally explore nature and the outdoor environment. Scientific inquiry provides opportunities to help children learn about life science. Here are some of the questions you might ask children in an everyday setting:

- Ask children to identify simple bugs and insects, such as a butterfly, a bee, a ladybug, and an ant.

- Ask children to describe parts of their bodies: head, face, nose, hands, feet, toes, tummy, and so on.

- When carrying a heavy object, like a wood block, say to children, "Look at how strong I am!" or "I have big muscles!"

- After children have been running, ask them to touch their chests to feel how fast their hearts are beating.

- Ask children to use magnifying glasses to observe the legs, wings, and antennae of grasshoppers and butterflies.

- Ask children to name animals from pictures in books.

- Ask children to identify which animals are the "mommies" and which ones are the "babies."

- Ask children to mimic the sounds different animals make.

- Ask children to identify groups of animals, such as farm, zoo, or forest animals.

- Ask children to identify the different habitats of living things, such as cows live on a farm.

Studying plants, animals, and humans is an important component of STEM education. It's important for children to know that most living things are dependent on the Earth for survival. Living things such as plants need soil, water, and light to grow. Animals and humans depend on the Earth for air, water, and food. Caregivers model respect for all living things and teach children the importance of caring for the Earth. Nature provides the perfect learning environment for learning about earth science.

Earth Science

Earth science is the study of observing and exploring the properties of earth materials such as soil, water, air, and rocks. Earth science also includes the movement and observable changes in the natural environment. This includes learning about the weather and seasons, as well as the sun, moon, and sky. For infants and young toddlers this might mean introducing basic information on the weather and wind. The caregiver might begin by talking about wind and how we need to bundle up or put on a jacket on a windy day. Here the caregiver might verbalize, "It's a windy day, so we're all going to put on our jackets before we go outside." Once outside, the caregiver might say, "I can feel the wind on my cheeks. I see the leaves moving in the wind." In this example, the child is being introduced to earth science in a natural setting. By connecting learning to real-life experiences, such as putting on a jacket on a windy day, caregivers allow children to build and connect learning as well as develop new schemas.

For older children, a caregiver might have them explore mixing water and sand together in a sandbox or pouring water on plants to help them grow. She could introduce physical science in this play experience too by talking about how the materials feel in the child's hand and how they change properties when water is added. Children are learning about the Earth through everyday hands-on experiences. Positive interactions, including self- and parallel talk, open-ended questions, paraphrasing, and prompts all support learning about earth science and STEM. Understanding the Earth and its properties profoundly influences children's learning about STEM.

Nature provides a natural classroom for children's learning. A child's curiosity is peaked in nature. Children begin to learn about the properties of earth materials as they play with and investigate natural objects. Exploring through their senses, children learn about the differences in the weight, color, texture, and shapes of objects such as rocks and sand. Playing with large rocks provides children with opportunities to see the unique characteristics of rocks while they begin to learn how to differentiate them. These skills not only promote understanding of earth science, but they are the beginning of the mathematical concepts of number sense, counting, sorting, and classification. The use of a simple tool such as a magnifying glass also promotes learning to differentiate between like objects. Through closer inspection, children begin to observe the fine details and characteristics of objects. This further expands children's knowledge and understanding of STEM.

Exploring outdoors promotes awareness of the changes in the sky and the seasons. Responsive caregivers might gesture to a baby or toddler when they see the cloud. They might say, "Look up at the blue sky. See the big white clouds." They might also say, "It's hot and very sunny today. We'll need to stay in the shade when we play outside." Outdoor environments provide caregivers with opportunities to see changes in the seasons too. Describe what you see outdoors and intentionally revisit trees and shrubs that change with the seasons. Trees that flower in the spring or go dormant in the winter provide wonderful opportunities to observe nature over time. Helping children see and explore the natural world is a key component of infant-toddler STEM education.

Everyday activities for earth science often incorporate physical science and life science. Many everyday activities provide opportunities for providers to teach across multiple science disciplines. As you plan earth science activities, consider what is developmentally appropriate for the age of the children in your care. Here are some examples of activities young children can do in both indoor and outdoor environments:

- Pour water on plants and watch them grow in the garden.

- Go for walks to gather fallen leaves and flowers.

- Observe the leaves on plants, using a magnifying glass.

- Play with buckets, shovels, and sieves in the sandbox.

- Mix and play with sand and water in the sandbox.

- Fill and pack wet sand into a mold to make a sand castle.

- Point out clouds in the sky and say, "Cloud."

- Point out and say, "Moon," when looking at the actual moon.

- Notice small bugs and insects on the ground and take care not to hurt or harm them.

Earth science provides many occasions to teach other STEM principles. There are a lot of great books, such as *Hello Ocean, Rainy Day, In the Sea, What Is the Weather Today?,* and *What Makes the Seasons?,* that teach young children about earth science. Caring and preserving the Earth is impor-tant for children to learn early through everyday experiences. I recommend you consider ways for children to learn about respecting the Earth. For example, use recycled materials for play and art activities. Provide special containers for recycling paper and plastic goods. Learning about the Earth and earth science is an important part of STEM learning.

TECHNOLOGY

The onset of digital technology and interactive media has changed our world dramatically. Digital technology is all around us, and most of us use one form or another every day. Today adults are faced with the profound question of what kind, if any, digital technology or media is appropriate for children under the age of eight. We know that our twenty-first-century learners will need access to digital technology as they prepare for the future, but when is it developmentally appropriate to introduce young children to it? The National Association for the Education of Young Children (NAEYC) and the Fred Rogers Center for Early Learning and Children's Media at Saint Vincent College provide guidance to adults through a joint position statement on digital technology and interactive media for children birth through age eight. In this position paper, it is recommended that children under the age of two have no exposure to screen media or screen time. Children over the age of two should have no more than one to two hours total per day (NAEYC 2012). They recommend that the use of digital technology should never be a passive activity for a young child. If digital technology is used, it must be done in context with adult interactions and be developmentally appropriate. These are well-researched guidelines and need to be followed when working with children birth to three years. When I think about technology for children under the age of three, I think about the evolution of technology and how simple machines and simple tools support children's learning about STEM.

Technology has been part of human history since the Stone Age, when humans first designed tools to make work and life easier. Early technology was designed primarily for survival and as a means to make hunting and food preparation more effective. When adults think of the use of technology, they typically think of computers, tablets, mobile devices, and interactive media. I like to refer to this kind of technology as the "Big T." So what kind of technology might we use in an infant-toddler early care setting to promote STEM? When I consider technology for infants, toddlers, and twos, I recommend technology in its simplest form: simple machines and simple tools.

Technology was first developed in the form of simple machines, which I call the "Little T" of technology. Remember the goal of technology is to make work and life easier. One of the first forms of technology was the invention of the wheel. The first machines were simple but effective forms of technology. Humans created six simple machines: inclined planes, wedges, pulleys, levers, wheels and axles, and screws. From

these first simple tools, thousands of useful tools and machines have been invented. Most of these tools or early technology is still used today. As humans needed tools to make life easier, people began to engineer or invent new technology. Engineering and technology work hand in hand. Engineers of today still use simple machines and simple tools to invent new technologies.

Simple machines are fundamental to the use of technology. Inclined planes can be seen in our early care environments every day. A playground slide or a walkway ramp is an example of an inclined plane. Wedges can be used to separate things, but also to hold them together. Some examples of wedges are shovels, knives, scissors, pushpins, and doorstops. Another simple machine is a pulley, which helps us lift heavy objects. A pulley's rope passes over a small wheel. When we pull down on one end of the rope, we lift a very heavy object tied to the other end. A lever allows us to move heavy objects or to open bottles and doors. Scissors, hammers, tongs, knives, and tweezers are all forms of levers. Wheels help things move and assist us in transferring heavy objects more easily. Gears are wheels with teeth that are used to speed up a machine or increase force. A pair of wheels is connected by an axle. The axle helps the wheels turn. Wheeled toys can be found easily in infant-toddler classrooms. Screws, although not used in play by young children, are equally as important in the design and construction of the classroom environment. Children's understanding of technology must also include the understanding of simple tools.

Simple tools, another form of the "Little T," are important for children's exploration and discovery. When investigating a bug or an insect, a magnifying glass allows the child to look more closely. A scale offers a child an opportunity to weigh objects to see which one is heavier. As older children investigate physical science, life science, and earth science, simple tools aid in the observations, investigations, and understanding about science. Simple tools include many everyday tools found in early learning environments and STEM learning centers. You will see the use of simple tools throughout the activities in this book. Here are just a few common simple tools that support STEM learning:

- scales
- classroom balances
- measuring cups
- measuring spoons
- scissors

- tweezers
- tongs
- magnifying glasses
- magnet wands
- rulers

- yardsticks
- measuring tapes
- eyedroppers
- funnels

- sieves
- spoons
- knives
- ice cream scoops

I recommend you include these simple tools in your early care settings. Take time to describe the tools, how they work, and how children can use them for investigation and discovery. Keep simple tools handy on walks and in outdoor play. For example, having a magnifying glass when a child discovers a bug or an insect outside will make the learning more fun and meaningful. Each interaction with simple machines and simple tools provides children with basic knowledge and understanding of how technology can be used. Keep in mind that simple tools and simple machines are often present in the books you read to young children. For example, *Rosie's Walk* and *The Little Mouse, the Red Ripe Strawberry, and the Big Hungry Bear* have several great illustrations of simple machines written into the stories. As you begin to recognize how often simple machines and simple tools, or the "Little Ts," are present in your classroom activities, the more you will include them in your everyday activities with children. You will see how useful they are in teaching children about the principles and concepts of STEM. As you learn more about simple machines and simple tools, you will see the important role engineering plays in STEM education.

ENGINEERING

Engineering is a process of solving problems. Engineers take steps to invent and create products or to find solutions to the problems around them. All areas of the Four Cs—critical thinking, communication, collaboration, and creativity—support the engineering process. Many inventions and solutions to problems use technology, including a variety of simple machines such as a ramps, levers, or screws, or simple tools such as scissors, tweezers, or magnifying glasses, to solve problems. As I said before, engineers work closely with technology to not only solve problems, but to make work and life easier. Children engage in engineering as they play and explore their world. Engineering is present in both indoor and outdoor environments where children build and create during play.

Early in life, young children begin solving problems and building. Cognitive skills and engineering work hand in hand. As children's cognitive skills increase, so does their ability to think, reason, and problem solve. Although their cognitive thinking skills are still developing, we see evidence of it in the children in our care. We see engineering when babies first begin to crawl. They may see a toy across the room that catches their attention. In order to get to the toy, they need to problem solve and navigate around other objects. In infant-toddler learning environments, babies and young toddlers begin playing with blocks and stacking cubes. These are early stages of engineering too. We often see toddlers sitting on the floor with a caregiver placing shapes in a sorting cube or a pegboard. Playing with bristle

blocks and soft foam blocks are also great ways to introduce infants and toddlers to engineering. As infants and toddlers explore soft blocks and stackable items, they gain an understanding of how to place one block on top of another to build and create structures. Here they are experiencing the physical science properties of balance, cause and effect, and gravity. As you work closely with young children, show your excitement about their efforts to build and stack toys. Comments such as "Wow! Look how high you stacked the blocks!" or "I see you are building a tall tower!" add to their enjoyment and enthusiasm in building. Blocks for infants and toddlers come in many forms, from foam to plastic to cardboard, all of which provide endless opportunities to invent, create, and build.

As children grow older and their play becomes more advanced, they may begin to build ramps. I've talked a lot about how children build on prior knowledge and experiences. With prior experience building, they've learned how high blocks can be placed before they topple over. With scaffolding from a caregiver, they've learned they can build a taller tower if they begin with a wider

base. A variety of materials can be used for older toddlers and twos as they increase their building experiences. Consider using recyclable materials and cardboard boxes for children's engineering activities. A child's imagination can turn a cardboard box into anything from a race car to a rocket ship. Through experiences with simple machines such as inclined planes and wheeled toys, children can extend their building and engineering knowledge. For example, when children add an incline or ramp to the structure, they learn that cars and trucks roll faster. As the incline is raised higher, the toys gain more speed. In this example, children are acquiring more experience with technology and simple machines as well as engineering. Books such as *Roll, Slope, and Slide: A Book about Ramps*, *Dig Dig Digging*, or *Goodnight, Goodnight, Construction Site* are great ways to demonstrate engineering to children. As children build and play with materials and learn about engineering, they are also gaining an understanding of mathematics.

MATHEMATICS

Children are born with an innate sense of math. They explore and discover the principles of mathematics through everyday experiences. Similar to other areas of STEM, the role of caregivers for infants and toddlers is to introduce children to the foundations of math. Children's mathematic understanding begins in the early years and develops over time. During the first three years of life, children learn about math informally. High-quality early care environments provide young children with a variety of hands-on, play-based experiences where they can begin to develop mathematical knowledge.

Like in many other areas of STEM education, cognitive development plays an important role in mathematical learning. We spoke earlier about cognitive development and children's interest in making sense of their world. As children's cognitive skills develop, they gain a better understanding of how things work. High-quality learning environments provide a variety of ongoing early learning experiences, which strengthen neural connections. As cognitive skills increase, children's understanding of mathematics develops. Moreover, cognitive skills become more advanced as young children build on prior knowledge. Therefore, responsive caregivers play an important role in increasing children's understanding of math by scaffolding their natural interests in math.

Number Sense and Operations

Learning about numbers is one of the primary concepts of mathematics. Number sense and operations includes understanding the relationships among numbers. This mathematical concept includes one-to-one correspondence, counting, addition and subtraction, quantification, and comparison of sets. What does this look like in an infant, toddler, and two early learning environment? Children learn one-to-one correspondence as they align or match one new item to the original set. Young children begin to understand this concept when they match all the "mama" bears together and all the "baby" bears together. When an older toddler plays with like items, such as farm animals, he might move or take away the lion. The child has learned that the lion belongs to the jungle animals and not to the farm animals set. Another example of number sense happens as children help at snacktime. A toddler or two-year-old who is helping set the table may count the napkins and place one napkin in front of each chair. Here the child is practicing not only counting but also one-to-one correspondence. Teaching number sense and operations is easy for caregivers once you know how to facilitate the mathematical concept in the early learning center.

Algebra: Patterns and Classification

Algebra is the understanding of patterns and classification of objects. Looking for patterns in nature is one of the first ways toddlers and twos learn about algebra. Many patterns exist in the leaves of trees, petals of flowers, and wings of butterflies. When caregivers explore earth science and life science, they introduce young children to myriad patterns. Patterns can be found throughout your classroom, including in the clothes children wear. Everyday objects, such as plastic animals, plastic fruit, and age-appropriate counting manipulatives, can be used for creating patterns. They are great for learning number sense and operations too! When creating patterns with older toddlers, ask them to identify the items in their pattern. For example, say, "Let's name the animals in your pattern." The child might respond, "I have a cow and a horse, a cow and a horse." As they learn to identify colors, they can advance their pattern identification by adding color words. For example, "I have a red apple, a yellow banana, a red apple and a yellow banana."

Young children identify and classify objects beginning in infancy. Classification is the ability to recognize, differentiate, and understand ideas and objects. As infants and toddlers explore their world through their senses, they quickly begin to classify and sort items mentally. People, objects, and ideas become stored as memory. Infants learn to recognize and differentiate familiar faces and voices of people in their lives. They learn early on what toys make sound and which toys roll or bounce. Although toddlers may not

fully understand the value of numbers, they are beginning to realize differences in categories and are able to recognize small sets of objects or subsets. Through interactions with responsive adults, children learn more-advanced categorization of objects. Young children are learning categories of objects, such as animals or cars. A young child may learn that dogs, cats, cows, or horses are also called animals. As their language skills develop, toddlers become more skilled at identifying, categorizing, and learning about subsets.

Children's ability to sort, group, and make connections between like or similar objects prepares them to develop more-complex math skills. Children will also use the skills of categorization as they learn to recognize and differentiate objects. In play-based learning environments, teachers plan activities where children can learn to sort, group, and make connections between like items. Teachers scaffold learning by providing similar objects for children to sort, such as large wood beads or the same-sized beads in different colors. Objects of different sizes provide toddlers with opportunities to learn the concepts of big and small. Sorting cubes provides opportunities for children to learn to sort items by shape and color. It's important to remember that children are learning about mathematics in the same way they learn about other areas of STEM—through play. Learning about patterns and classification should be done through everyday activities and with the guidance of responsive caregiving.

Geometry: Shapes and Spatial Relationships

Geometry is learning about shapes and spatial relationships. Developing the concepts of spatial relationships begins in infancy. Within a few months of life, infants' vision becomes clearer and they begin to watch and observe how things move. They might see the objects on a mobile move and change direction as the pieces touch each other. As they explore objects with their mouths and move and manipulate toys, they are learning about the properties of spatial relation-

ships. Not only are babies learning about spatial relationships, but they are learning about physical science too! Through sensorimotor exploration young children begin to recognize that some objects or surfaces are smooth while others may be rough or bumpy. Through trial and error, they learn how items fit together and how things open and close. They may play with puzzle pieces or soft blocks. There are a variety of play mats that provide infants with objects to move and rotate as they learn spatial relationships.

Responsive caregivers provide child-directed activities, toys, and objects for infants and toddlers to learn about spatial relationships. Not only are children learning about the spatial properties of objects, they are learning about their own bodies and their own physical space. Here they are learning about life science too! As children become mobile, caregivers can provide interesting things for children to crawl through and over. These hands-on experiences help children learn how their bodies fit and squeeze into spaces. Responsive caregivers use language and verbal cues to acknowledge the child's efforts to navigate the environmental space, supporting the child's growing ability to learn about spatial relationships. Each new toy or object provides new opportunities for young children to learn and explore the world around them.

Measurement and Mathematical Reasoning

Children learn about measurement as they play and explore. At this stage of development, young children are learning to understand measurement, such as big or little, more or less, some or more, and hot and cold. Through play, children engage in informal assessment of measurement. As they dip their hands in a sink of water, they learn about the differences in temperature and if the water is hot or cold. Intuitively they know which cookie is bigger and when a cup is empty. Asking "More please!" demonstrates a child's understanding of more or less. As children build and stack building blocks or stackable toys, they

are learning the physical properties of height and which tower is higher. Through everyday experiences, children learn about weight. For example, a child senses that a bucket with water feels heavy as he carries it to the sand area. He gains a sense of weight as he lifts up the empty bucket, noticing that it feels different or lighter. In this example, a responsive caregiver might say to the child, "I see you carrying that heavy bucket to the sand. Does it feel different without the water? Does it feel lighter than before?"

Mathematical reasoning is another key component of learning. Mathematical reasoning encompasses all areas of mathematics, including number sense and operations, patterns, classification, shapes, spatial relationships, and measurement. As children's cognitive skills increase, their ability to think, reason, and problem solve increases. Keep in mind that books, songs, and chants are also a great way to teach and reinforce mathematical reasoning. Each activity in this book includes a list of suggested books for you to read to support children's STEM learning. Songs like "Five Little Monkeys Jumping on the Bed," "Ten in the Bed," or "Five Little Speckled Frogs" are great ways to engage children in learning mathematics. As you responsively interact with young children, their natural interest and curiosity about the world grows.

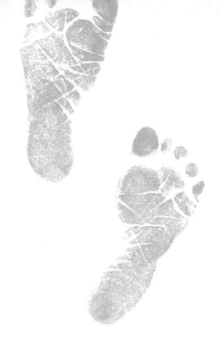

PART

4

STEM Activities

The activities in this book are designed to promote STEM learning for infants and toddlers. Some activities lend themselves better to infants rather than toddlers, or toddlers rather than twos. Knowing the children in your care will help you determine which activities you select and how to modify them for each child. Each of the activities includes the following information:

- Recommended Ages
- STEM Concepts: Science, Technology, Engineering, Math
- Learning Outcomes
- Teaching Tips
- Materials
- Getting Ready
- How To
- Expand the Activity
- Build Vocabulary
- Inquiry Questions and Comments
- Home-School Connection
- Suggested Books

HOW TO USE THESE ACTIVITIES

The activities that follow are ordered alphabetically by title. At the beginning of each activity, shaded bullets indicate whether the activity is intended for infants, toddlers, or twos. Shaded bullets also identify the STEM concepts each activity covers. For example, All the Pretty Little Flowers is for toddlers and twos, and the activity incorporates science, technology, and math concepts. You can utilize the indexes at the end of the book to view activities by STEM concept (page 177) or by the age of the child (page 179). Caregivers can select or adapt activities to meet the developmental needs of any child, including children with special needs. Each activity targets specific STEM learning and development opportunities. "Getting Ready" addresses what should be prepped ahead of time. Hints for making it easier to prepare for the activity are also included.

How-to instructions and ways to expand the learning opportunities are included with the activities. Since language development is essential for early learning, all of the activities have a list of recommended vocabulary words, questions, and prompts to use with children. The home-school connection is important in supporting children's learning. Suggestions for home learning opportunities are included with each activity. Suggested books can be added to meet the needs and interests of the children and support the STEM learning process. The activities are designed to be played during indoor and outdoor time. Since many classrooms have mixed-age groups, caregivers may need to modify the activity to meet the developmental stage of the children in their classroom.

Most of the materials called for in the activities are commonly found in child care settings, including crayons, markers, liquid glue, glue sticks, glue gun, yarn, construction paper, scissors, and so on. Other items such as large plastic tubs, sponges, easels, paint, paintbrushes, stamps, and stamp pads are also used. You will find a list of STEM-related materials on pages 26–27. Modifications for expanding the activity include additional materials if needed. Be sure the materials suggested in modifications for the activity are age appropriate and the children can use them safely. Remember to select materials that are nontoxic and safe for infants and toddlers. You will also need to modify the materials if children have food allergies. Again, activities that involve water must be closely supervised and may not be appropriate for infants and young toddlers.

Resources to support the activities are listed in the back of the book, along with a comprehensive list of suggested STEM books. As you begin planning and implementing these activities into your program, remember that each child is unique. Children learn best in environments where they are loved, cared for, and valued as unique individuals. Highly qualified early childhood professionals commit to program excellence, providing STEM learning environments that optimize children's learning potential.

All the Pretty Little Flowers

Ages

○ **Infants**

● **Toddlers**

● **Twos**

STEM Concepts

● **Science** (Life science, Earth science)

● **Technology** (Simple tools)

○ **Engineering**

● **Math** (Patterns and classification)

Learning Outcomes

Children will explore the outdoor environment and collect leaves and flowers that have fallen on the ground. Children can learn about life and earth science through nature walks and exploration.

Teaching Tips

Through nature walks, you can help children differentiate between living and nonliving things and learn the life cycle of living things such as trees, plants, and flowers.

Materials

• plastic storage bags

• 2 or 3 magnifying glasses

• plastic trays

Getting Ready

No additional preparation is needed.

How To

Go on a nature walk, taking with you a large plastic storage bag and two or three magnifying glasses. Older children can carry their own bags for collecting items. As you walk, talk to the children about what you see and hear. If you see bugs or insects, stop and investigate what you observe. Use a magnifying glass for closer examination of the natural materials (living and nonliving) you see. Collect flowers and leaves that have fallen on the ground and place them in the storage bag. After the walk, talk to the children about their experience. Place all the items on one or two plastic trays for sorting and classifying. Invite the children to use the magnifying glasses to investigate the materials closely to look for the differences in the natural materials.

Hint: The observation discussion can be done either indoors or outdoors.

Expand the Activity

Ask older children to sort the materials into different categories, such as twigs, leaves, flower petals, or stems. Ask open-ended questions about what they observe.

Build Vocabulary

nature, walk, tree, plant, bush, flower, petal, twig, leaf, magnify, magnifying glass, investigate

Inquiry Questions and Comments

- What do you see when you look through the magnifying glass?

- How many natural materials did we find? Let's count them.

- What does the leaf feel like?

- How does it feel different than this twig?

- What are the differences between this leaf and the other one?

Home-School Connection

Have children draw a picture at school about what they experienced on the nature walk. Ask parents to document what their child says. Invite parents to use the child's picture to guide their conversation about what the child experienced on the nature walk.

Suggested Books

- *Are You a Bee?* by Judy Allen

- *Are You a Butterfly?* by Judy Allen

- *Are You a Ladybug?* by Judy Allen

- *Bugs* by Andrews McMeel Publishing

- *Counting in the Garden* by Kim Parker

- *I Love Bugs* by Philemon Sturges

- *In the Tall, Tall Grass* by Denise Fleming

- *Planting a Rainbow* by Lois Ehlert

- *The Surprise Garden* by Zoe Hall

Baby Bubble Fun

Ages

● **Infants**

● **Toddlers**

○ **Twos**

STEM Concepts

● **Science** (Physical science)

● **Technology** (Simple tools)

○ **Engineering**

● **Math** (Shapes)

Learning Outcomes

Children will explore the physical properties of water and the elasticity and shape of bubbles.

Teaching Tips

Bubbles provide the opportunity to study the science concepts of elasticity, surface tension, chemistry, and light. Children will engage in processes of observation and experimentation by playing with bubbles.

Materials

• liquid bubble soap

• water

• large tub or an empty sensory table

• heavy-duty paint aprons or smocks

• towels

Getting Ready

No additional preparation is needed.

How To

Place a small amount of liquid bubble soap in the bottom of the tub and fill with water. Swish your hands around to make as many bubbles as possible. Let the children watch as you make the bubbles. Show the children how you can lift the bubbles up and make mounds and small sculptures. Demonstrate how you can squeeze the bubbles between your fingers. Invite a few children at a time to play and create bubble sculptures. Show the children how to blow on the bubbles and watch how they float in the air.

Expand the Activity

Place toys such as a rubber duck, baby doll, plastic manipulative, or plastic farm animal in the water. Let the children experiment with items that float and sink.

Build Vocabulary

bubbles, wet, water, liquid, swish, float, soft, graceful, cold, tub, squeeze, front, back, hands, fingers

Inquiry Questions and Comments

• I'm going to put the liquid bubble soap in the tub.

• Watch as I make the bubbles by swishing the water around with my hands.

- Look at how I squeeze the bubbles with my hands.

- Who wants to join me?

- What do you feel? I feel the soft bubbles.

- Do your hands feel wet?

- Look how the bubbles can get taller.

Home-School Connection

Invite parents to purchase or make their own bubble solution. Parents can pour the bubble solution into a flat tray and experiment with making bubbles by using household utensils.

Suggested Books

- *Bubble Bath Baby* by Libby Ellis

- *The Bubble Factory* by Tomie De Paola

- *Bubbles, Bubbles* by Kathi Appelt

- *Bubbles, Bubbles* by Sesame Street

- *Bubble Trouble* by Margaret Mahy

- *My Five Senses* by Aliki

- *My Five Senses* by Margaret Miller

Balancing Act: Noodle Fun

Ages

○ **Infants**
● **Toddlers**
● **Twos**

STEM Concepts

● **Science** (Physical science, Life science)
○ **Technology**
○ **Engineering**
○ **Math**

Learning Outcomes

Children will gain experience with balance as they experiment with how to keep something upright and balanced.

Teaching Tips

Children experiment with balance and motion as they learn how to adjust their bodies to maintain balance of an object while moving.

Materials

• foam pool noodles

• scissors

Getting Ready

Cut noodles into four equal pieces. For older children, cut one noodle in half.

How To

Model for children how to balance the noodle horizontally in the palm of your hand, then have the children balance the noodle horizontally in one hand. Toddlers may want to use two hands at first. Explain how they need to place one hand in the middle of the noodle to stabilize it. Have them walk around the room. Next, model for them balancing a noodle vertically in one hand; this will require more concentration and balance. Remind them that they can use their other hand for stability. Have the children walk around trying to balance the noodle in one hand. Explain to the children how they are "balancing" the noodle in their hands.

Hint: The smaller the noodle the easier it will be for children to balance. Children will be focused on the noodle(s) in their hands, so be sure there is plenty of open space that is free of obstacles for children to practice balancing. This is a fun activity to do outside.

Expand the Activity

- Cut a full-size noodle in half lengthwise and ask children to try to walk along the length of the noodle to begin gaining a sense of balance. Demonstrate how they might use their arms to help them balance. Don't worry if the children find this hard to do; adults have trouble with this activity too! Children are developing the concept of balance.

- Place a piece of painter's tape 5–6 feet long on the ground and have children practice walking along the tape. You can make zigzag lines and shapes from the tape too!

Build Vocabulary

balance, stabilize, adjust, adjustment, movement, palm, feet, body, concentration, fast, slow

Inquiry Questions and Comments

- We're going to learn about balance today. Let's practice balancing on one foot. Great! Sometimes we have to hop a little in order to keep our balance.

- Now we're going to try balancing something in our hand. This is the palm of your hand. Show me the palm of your hand. Place the noodle (horizontally) across the palm of your hand.

- What happens when you move your other hand?

- How can you keep the noodle in your hand?

- What happens when you move fast?

- What happens when you move slowly?

Home-School Connection

Share with parents that you introduced the concept of balance to the children today. Invite the parents to find household objects that the children can use to practice learning about balance and how to stabilize objects.

Suggested Books

- *Barnyard Dance* by Sandra Boynton
- *Dancing Feet* by Lindsey Craig
- *From Head to Toe* (board book) by Eric Carle
- *My First Body* by DK Publishing

Ball Painting

Ages

○ Infants

○ Toddlers

● Twos

STEM Concepts

● **Science** (Physical science, Life science)

○ **Technology**

○ **Engineering**

○ **Math**

Learning Outcomes

Children will gain an understanding of motion, cause and effect, and blending colors as they lift the sides of a plastic swimming pool.

Teaching Tips

The motion of the balls will mix the colors together.

Materials

• small plastic swimming pool

• white butcher paper

• scissors

• masking tape

• liquid watercolor paints

• 4 or 5 different-size rubber balls

• bucket with soap and water for cleanup

Getting Ready

Purchase a small plastic swimming pool if needed.

How To

Cut butcher paper to fit the bottom of the swimming pool and extend up the sides. Place a loop of folded-over tape in the middle and along the sides of the pool to help secure the paper. Place different colors of liquid watercolor paint on the paper. Let the children place the balls in the swimming pool. Ask three or four children at a time to hold on to the edge of the pool and help roll the ball back and forth. Children will gain a sense of their own bodies as they lift and lower the sides of the pool. Repeat the activity with clean paper so another group of children can join in the fun.

Hint: This can be a bit messy, so have children wear play clothes for this activity. Have buckets of soap and water handy for cleanup.

Expand the Activity

Remove the balls and leave the painted paper inside the pool. Capture the children's footprints by asking three or four children to stand inside the pool. Brush liquid watercolor on their feet. Help them step out of the pool and walk on new pieces of white paper to capture their footprints.

Build Vocabulary

paint, balls, roll, lift, muscles, hands, watch, blend, colors, pool

Inquiry Questions and Comments

- What colors of paint should we use?

- Which balls should we use?

- What happens when we lift up the edges of the pool?

- What happens to the paint as the balls roll back and forth?

- How high can we roll the balls up the edges?

- We're working together to move the balls over the paper.

Home-School Connection

Invite parents to repeat this activity using the top of a large box and small balls. Children will have a similar experience, but on a smaller scale.

Suggested Books

- *Baby Touch and Feel: Colors and Shapes* by DK Publishing

- *Bright Baby Colors, ABC, and Numbers First Words* by Roger Priddy

- *First 100 Numbers Colors Shapes (Bright Baby)* by Roger Priddy

- *My Five Senses* by Aliki

- *My Five Senses* by Margaret Miller

- *White Rabbit's Color Book* by Alan Baker

Barnyard Buddies

Ages

○ Infants

● Toddlers

● Twos

STEM Concepts

● **Science** (Physical science, Life science, Earth science)

○ **Technology**

○ **Engineering**

● **Math** (Number sense and operations, Classification)

Learning Outcomes

Children will gain knowledge of the characteristics of farm animals and a deeper understanding of the life cycle. Children will practice counting and sorting farm animals and learn about living things.

Teaching Tips

Farm animals are living things. A variety of animals live on farms, including horses, cows, chickens, ducks, and goats. Each animal makes a different sound. They live in a variety of different habitats. For example, horses sleep in a stable, goats live in a pen, cows in a shed, ducks in a pond, and chickens in a coop. They each have characteristics that are unique to them.

Materials

• storybooks about farms

• plastic farm animals of different sizes

• toy farm set with barns, tractors, and other farm items

• small building blocks

• blue construction paper

• scissors

• tape

Getting Ready

Read and discuss books about the farm. Introduce the different animals on the farm, what sounds they make, and where they live (habitat) on the farm. On the day of the activity, set up a play area on a table for the farm. Use small building blocks to form pens and stables for animals that live in barns. Cut a piece of blue construction paper for a duck pond. Tape the paper to the table and place rubber ducks on it. Arrange the farm and place animals throughout the play area.

How To

Introduce the children to the different habitats you have created on the farm. Let the children explore these materials.

Expand the Activity

- Ask the children to sort and count the farm animals.

- Modify the dramatic play area into a farm. Place pictures of real farm animals on the walls of the dramatic play area. Cover the kitchen set with red construction paper to make it look like a barn. Add straw hats and red scarves for dress-up.

Build Vocabulary

farm, barn, pen, stable, pond, names of the farm animals

Inquiry Questions and Comments

- What animals are on our farm?

- How could we build a barn for the animals?

- Are there more horses or cows on the farm?

- How many cows are there?

- What animal lives in the barn?

Home-School Connection

Invite parents to discuss farm animals, the sounds they make, and where they might live on a farm. Encourage parents to read books about farm life and sing "Old Macdonald Had a Farm," with their child.

Suggested Books

- *Barnyard Dance* by Sandra Boynton

- *Big Red Barn* by Margaret Wise Brown

- *Bright Baby Touch and Feel Baby Animals* by Roger Priddy

- *Farm Animals* by Phoebe Dunn

- *Mrs. Wishy-Washy's Farm* by Joy Cowley

- *Open the Barn Door* by Christopher Santoro

- *Pete the Cat: Old MacDonald Had a Farm* by James Dean

Beautiful Butterflies

Ages

○ **Infants**
● **Toddlers**
● **Twos**

STEM Concepts

● **Science** (Life Science, Earth Science)
● **Technology** (Simple Tools)
○ **Engineering**
● **Math** (Patterning, Measurement)

Learning Outcomes

Children gain an understanding of the life cycle of a butterfly. They will observe different patterns seen on butterfly wings.

Teaching Tips

Explain the life cycle of a butterfly, including how caterpillars feed on leaves, the formation of the cocoon-like chrysalis, and wing formation. Also describe parts of the butterfly such as the antennae. Look for butterflies outdoors or on a nature walk. Read the suggested books and show photographs of the life cycle to the children.

Materials

• egg cartons
• scissors
• construction paper
• green chenille stems
• awl
• books and photographs of butterflies
• markers and/or crayons
• glue

Getting Ready

Cut the cover off of the egg cartons and then cut the bottoms lengthwise to make two "bumpy" caterpillar bodies. Cut the green chenille stems to about 4 inches in length. Poke holes for the antennae in the egg cartons using an awl or another sharp object.

How To

Show the children pictures of butterflies. Read the suggested books to the children. Take a walk to see if you can observe butterflies. Talk to them about the patterns and colors of the butterfly's wings. Talk about the life cycle of butterflies and what caterpillars look like.

Let the children color the egg cartons with markers or crayons and cover them with pieces of construction paper. Older children will be able to place the green chenille stems into the holes to make the antennae. Use black markers to make the eyes of the caterpillar. Place the caterpillars around the classroom for decoration.

Expand the Activity

1. Make the body of the butterfly by cutting brown construction paper into the shape of a long oval with a round circle for the head.

2. Cover a table with butcher paper. Paint the palms of the children's hands and show them

how to place their handprints close together with fingertips pointing outward on the paper to make the wings of the butterfly.

3. After the paint has dried, cut out the handprints and glue on the brown body of the butterfly.

4. Curl the wings inward to add depth to the butterfly.

5. Fold chenille stems in half and glue them to the head.

6. Use fishing line to hang the butterflies from the ceiling near a window so it looks as if they are flying.

Build Vocabulary

butterfly, insect, caterpillar, wings, eggs, leaves, fly, colors, patterns

Inquiry Questions and Comments

• We're going to look at pictures and read a story about butterflies. Butterflies are beautiful insects. They fly from flower to flower. There are different kinds of butterflies. They have different colors and patterns. What do you see when you look at this butterfly?

• How does the caterpillar move?

• What does the caterpillar eat?

Home-School Connection

Send each child home with a paper plate and one craft stick. Ask parents to have the children color the paper plates with crayons or markers. Instruct parents to cut the colored paper plate in half and cut the round edges to make wings. Use a marker to draw a smiley face on the top of the craft stick. Attach the wings to the craft stick with glue to make the butterfly.

Suggested Books

• *Are You a Butterfly?* by Judy Allen

• *Magnificent Monarchs* by Linda Glaser

• *Monarch and Milkweed* by Helen Frost

• *Monarch Butterfly* by Gail Gibbons

• *National Geographic Little Kids First Big Book of Bugs* by Catherine Hughes

• *The Very Hungry Caterpillar* by Eric Carle

Boat Float

Ages

○ **Infants**

○ **Toddlers**

● **Twos**

STEM Concepts

● **Science** (Physical science)

○ **Technology**

● **Engineering** (Engineering)

● **Math** (Number sense and operations, Measurement, Mathematical reasoning)

Learning Outcomes

Children will gain experience building and designing their own boat and testing it to see if the boat has buoyancy.

Teaching Tips

Objects either sink or float depending upon the object's density and mass. Objects that are denser than water will sink, whereas objects with less mass (than water) will float. Buoyancy is the force that makes an object remain floating instead of sinking when placed in water.

Materials

• clear plastic storage box, such as one for storing sweaters

• water

• aluminum foil

• scissors

• variety of small plastic toys such as cars, animals, or other small objects

Getting Ready

Fill the plastic box halfway full with water. Cut aluminum foil into 6-inch squares.

How To

Explain to the children that they will be building boats today using aluminum foil. The aluminum boats will float on top of the water. Model how to design a boat by bending up the edges of the foil to provide a lip on the boat. Remind the children that foil can easily tear, so they will need to have "gentle hands" when they are constructing their boats. Let the children place their boats in the water when they are done to see if they float. Once they have tested to see if their boat floats, invite them to add two or three (or more) plastic animals to see how many animals the boat can hold before sinking.

Hint: If the edges of the boat are higher, the boat will hold more objects.

Expand the Activity

• Invite the children to hold one penny in their right hand. In their left hand, add a few more pennies, one at a time. Ask them which hand feels heavier and which one is lighter. Add the pennies one at a time to the boats to see if they sink or float.

• Count the items as you place them in the boat. Graph how many objects each child added before the boat sank.

Build Vocabulary

aluminum foil, square, boat, sink, float, water, construct, design, animals

Inquiry Questions and Comments

- I am using gentle hands to construct my boat. We want to fold the edges of the boat up to form a lip on the boat. This will help it stay afloat.

- You're working hard on your boats. I can see you are thinking about different ways to construct them.

- It's okay if your boat didn't float. You can try again.

- How might you change or design the edges to keep your boat afloat? Let's see if it will float better now.

- What if we add farm animals to your boat? Do you think it will still float?

- How many animals do you think it will take to sink your boat? Let's see.

Home-School Connection

Invite parents to make an aluminum foil boat at home with their child. They can test it out during bath time. They can also look for other objects at home that sink or float.

Suggested Books

- *Boats* by Anne Rockwell

- *Boats Board Book* by Byron Barton

- *Sally in the Sand* by Stephen Huneck

- *Who Sank the Boat?* By Pamela Allen

Brush and Sponge Art

Ages

○ **Infants**

○ **Toddlers**

● **Twos**

STEM Concepts

● **Science** (Physical science, Life science, Earth science)

○ **Technology**

○ **Engineering**

● **Math** (Number sense and operations)

Learning Outcomes

Children will use their senses to explore different natural and manufactured sponges.

Teaching Tips

Natural sponges grow in all different shapes and sizes. Sea sponges and loofahs are both natural sponges. The sea sponge grows in the ocean. A loofah is a fruit, similar to a cucumber, and grows on a vine. The loofah is very fibrous and can be used for scrubbing in bathrooms and kitchens.

Materials

• large easel paper or white construction paper

• tempera paint in different colors

• flat containers for paint

• variety of clean, dry sponges, including sea sponges, loofahs, and kitchen sponges

• variety of clean, dry brushes, including scrub brushes

Getting Ready

No additional preparation needed.

How To

Let the children feel and explore the sponges and brushes before you start the art activity. Explain how natural sponges grow in nature. A variety of sponges and brushes will add different textures and interest to the children's art. Place paint in flat containers or on the easel stand and let the children paint with the sponges and brushes. Using one color at a time, help children learn the name of the color. This activity can be done using an easel or on a small table, either as an indoor or outdoor activity.

Expand the Activity

• Model how to use scrub brushes with stiff bristles and how to splatter the paint. Add other objects, such as a flyswatter, a small strainer, or a slotted spatula to use in painting.

• Use two primary colors at a time and talk to the child about how two colors create a new color. For example, red and yellow make orange. Small groups of children can work side by side sharing the paint, sponges, and brushes.

Build Vocabulary

paint, easel, paper, sponges, loofah, scrub brushes, bristles, color

Inquiry Questions and Comments

- Today, we're going to explore and paint with different sponges and brushes. Some of these brushes and sponges you might see at home. I'll pass them around so you can touch and feel them.

- What does this one feel like? How about this one?

- Do they feel the same or different?

- I have set up a painting area with red paint. You can paint with the sponges and brushes. Each one will make a different pattern on the paper.

- Which one do you like the best?

Home-School Connection

Ask parents to let children explore with clean, dry brushes and sponges they have in their homes.

Suggested Books

- *Bright Baby Colors, ABC, and Numbers* by Roger Priddy

- *First 100 Numbers Colors Shapes (Bright Baby)* by Roger Priddy

- *My Hands* by Aliki

- *Sally in the Sand* by Stephen Huneck

- *Under the Sea* by Anna Milbourne

- *Way Deep in the Deep Blue Sea* by Jan Peck

- *White Rabbit's Color Book* by Alan Baker

Bubble Wands

Ages

○ **Infants**

○ **Toddlers**

● **Twos**

STEM Concepts

● **Science** (Physical science, Life science, Earth science)

● **Technology** (Simple tools)

● **Engineering** (Engineering)

● **Math** (Shapes)

Learning Outcomes

Children will learn how to engineer a homemade bubble wand. They will explore the properties of physical, life, and earth science. Children will blow the soapy solution through the wands using their breath.

Teaching Tips

A bubble is a thin film of soapy water filled with air. Bubbles can pop for several reasons, including hitting a dry surface, being broken by a strong wind, or having the air inside the bubble evaporate.

Materials

• water

• dishwashing soap

• eggbeater

• measuring cup

• tablespoon

• plastic bucket

• colorful chenille stems

• coat hangers

• duct tape

• containers to hold bubble solution

• glycerin (found in drug stores), optional

• corn syrup, optional

• towels for cleanup

Getting Ready

The bubble solution is best if it's made the day before. To make the bubbles solution, mix 1 cup

of water and 2 tablespoons of dishwashing soap in the plastic bucket. Beat the mixture with the eggbeater.

How To

Invite the children to watch and help you make the bubble wands. Take a chenille stem and twist the ends together to make a circle. Wind another chenille stem around it to make the handle. For a larger wand, twist two chenille stems together or cover the neck of a wire coat hanger with duct tape and reshape it into a star, circle, square, or diamond. The children can select the color of chenille stems and help hold them as you bend the ends into a shape.

Pour the bubble solution into individual containers. Dip the wands into the soapy solution. Demonstrate for younger children how to blow into the soapy wand. Describe the bubbles and let the children play.

Hint: You can add 1–2 tablespoons of either corn syrup or glycerin for a different bubble experience. This activity can get messy and is best done outdoors on a sunny day.

Expand the Activity

For more bubble fun and exploration, use other household items such as flyswatters, plastic berry baskets, slotted spoons, and plastic cookie cutters to make different-sized bubbles.

Build Vocabulary

bubbles, soapy solution, wand, chenille stem, twist, float, pop, clear, dip

Inquiry Questions and Comments

- Today you are going to help me make bubble wands.
- We can make the wands into different shapes.
- What color chenille stem should we use?
- Watch as I twist the wand into a shape like a heart.
- What shape do you want me to make?
- What happens as we place the wand in the soapy water?
- What happens when the wind blows the bubble?
- Let's watch it and see how far it will float in the sky.

Home-School Connection

Invite parents to repeat the activity at home using household items.

Suggested Books

- *Brown Rabbit's Shape Book* by Alan Baker
- *Baby Touch and Feel: Colors and Shapes* by DK Publishing
- *Bubble Bath Baby* by Libby Ellis
- *The Bubble Factory* by Tomie De Paola
- *Bubbles, Bubbles* by Kathi Appelt
- *Bubbles, Bubbles* by Sesame Street
- *Bubble Trouble* by Margaret Mahy
- *First 100 Numbers Colors Shapes (Bright Baby)* by Roger Priddy
- *My Five Senses* by Aliki
- *My Five Senses* by Margaret Miller
- *Shapes, Shapes, Shapes* by Tana Hoban

Bubble Worms

Ages

○ **Infants**

○ **Toddlers**

● **Twos**

STEM Concepts

● **Science** (Physical science, Life science)

● **Technology** (Simple tools)

○ **Engineering**

● **Math** (Shapes)

Learning Outcomes

Children will explore life science and their ability to use their lungs to blow air bubbles. They will also learn about the physical properties of water and the elasticity and shapes of bubbles.

Teaching Tips

Bubbles provide the opportunity to study science concepts such as elasticity, surface tension, chemistry, and light. Children will engage in processes of observation and experimentation by playing with bubbles.

Materials

• several clean, empty 8-ounce plastic water bottles

• scissors

• several medium-size socks (they will need to fit snugly around the bottom of the water bottles)

• dishwashing soap

• water

• measuring cup

• small bowl or storage container

Getting Ready

Use scissors to cut off the bottom of each water bottle. The edges may be sharp, so don't allow the children to handle the bottle until the sock is placed snugly around the bottom of the water bottle. Practice blowing with the children before starting this activity by having them place their hands in front of their mouth as they blow. This will give them the experience of feeling the air blowing out from their lungs.

How To

1. Pull a sock over the bottom of each water bottle to cover the cut-off edge. Pull the sock up toward the top of the bottle. If you have enough sock, fold over the top edge to give the sock a cuff. This will help secure it in place. If the sock is too big, you can secure it with a rubber band.

2. Combine ¼ cup of dishwashing soap with ½ cup of water in the bowl or container. Swirl to mix.

3. Dip the bottom of the bottle in the bubble solution, allowing the bottom of the sock to get nice and soapy. Have the children blow into the top of the bottle to release the bubbles. It should make a long snake-like bubble.

Expand the Activity

- Add food coloring to the soapy water.

- Informally measure to see who can make the longest bubble "worm."

Build Vocabulary

bubbles, bottle, sock, tight, cut, soft, wet, water, liquid, soapy, graceful, hands, blow

Inquiry Questions and Comments

- Let's pull the sock over the bottom of the bottle. Be sure it's nice and tight.

- Who would like to help me pour the dishwashing soap into the container?

- Who would like to help me pour the water into the container?

- What does the soapy liquid feel like?

- Do your hands feel wet?

- We're going to dip the bottom of the bottle into the soapy water.

- Watch me as I blow through the hole. Now you try!

Home-School Connection

Invite parents to purchase or make their own bubble solution. Parents can pour the bubble solution into a flat tray and experiment making bubbles with household utensils.

Suggested Books

- *The Bubble Factory* by Tomie De Paola

- *Bubbles, Bubbles* by Kathi Appelt

- *Bubbles, Bubbles* by Sesame Street

- *Bubble Trouble* by Margaret Mahy

- *My Five Senses* by Aliki

- *My Five Senses* by Margaret Miller

Build a Bridge

Ages

○ **Infants**

○ **Toddlers**

● **Twos**

STEM Concepts

● **Science** (Physical science)

● **Technology** (Simple tool)

● **Engineering** (Engineering)

● **Math** (Number sense and operations, Spatial relationships, Measurement, Mathematical reasoning)

Learning Outcomes

Children will design and build a bridge to gain an understanding of engineering. They will experience the process of testing and retesting their theories.

Teaching Tips

A bridge is a structure built over a river, road, or railway that allows people and vehicles to move across an open space. Bridges are designed to hold weight and need anchors on either end to help support the deck.

Materials

• 3 or 4 pieces of 8½ × 11–inch colored card stock

• scissors

• masking or duct tape

• 2 wood building blocks, each at least 5½ × 1⅜ × 2¾ inches or larger

• coins, counting bears, pom-poms, or other small objects to place on top of the bridge

• charting paper

• markers

Getting Ready

Cut one piece of card stock in quarter strips.

How To

Share with the children that you are going to build a bridge out of paper. Explain to the children that they can use the large uncut pieces of paper or the smaller strips of paper to build their bridge. Ask the children to help you place and tape the paper of their choice on the blocks. Separate the blocks so the paper is taut and parallel to the table. Let the children touch and examine the items you are going to place on the bridge. Ask them to informally weigh the objects using their hands to see which ones feel light and which ones feel heavy. Ask them to predict which items the bridge will hold best. Chart their ideas on paper.

Have children place the lighter items, like pom-poms, on the bridge first. Count them as the children place them on the bridge. Chart how many items the paper bridge held before it collapsed. Next repeat the process using heavier objects. Discuss with the children the differences between the materials and what happened when they were placed on the bridge. Place support in the middle of the bridge and repeat the activity. Discuss and chart the results. Document their bridge designs with photographs.

Hint: Be sure to spend some time talking and reading to children about bridges before starting this activity. You can also twist and refold the paper as you experiment with how to build a stronger bridge out of paper. For example, accordion-folded paper is stronger than a flat piece of paper. Be sure to closely supervise young children to make sure they don't place small objects in their mouths.

Expand the Activity

- Use additional materials such as cardboard strips, Styrofoam, or wood blocks to build different kinds of bridges. Talk to the children about the differences in materials and ask them why they think one material might be stronger than another.

- Talk to the children about placing materials under the bridge for stability and added strength. Test their predictions.

Build Vocabulary

build, design, strength, weight, support, stability, blocks, paper, tape, anchor, count, collapse

Inquiry Questions and Comments

- We're going to design a bridge today out of paper and wood blocks. The blocks will help anchor the paper. We're going to place items on the bridge to see how many the bridge will hold.

- Which item feels heavy? Which one feels light?

- Let's count how many pom-poms can go on the bridge before it collapses.

- How could we support the bridge to make it stronger?

- Let's see if it helps if we put a piece of paper under the middle of the bridge.

- What happened?

Home-School Connection

Invite parents to point out bridges and overpasses as they drive in the car. Let children play with materials at home to create bridges.

Suggested Books

- *Bridges: Amazing Structures to Design, Build, & Test* by Carol A. Johmann

- *The World's Most Amazing Bridges* by Michael Hurley

Build and Tumble

Ages

○ **Infants**

● **Toddlers**

● **Twos**

STEM Concepts

● **Science** (Physical science)

○ **Technology**

● **Engineering** (Engineering)

● **Math** (Spatial relationships, Measurement, Mathematical reasoning)

Learning Outcomes

Children will gain experience with building and number sense as they play with blocks. Through this activity, children will learn spatial relationships, gravity, balance, and problem solving.

Teaching Tips

Building is a process of engineering where children learn about spatial awareness, gravity, balance, and problem solving. They are also learning about trial and error.

Materials

• stackable soft foam or cardboard blocks

• hollow wood blocks for older children, optional

Getting Ready

No additional preparation is needed.

How To

On a flat surface, model how to stack soft blocks. Invite children to begin building themselves. If needed, stack a few blocks by yourself and then invite children to add on to your structure. Children are quick to learn how to build structures. Half the fun is watching the blocks tumble to the ground. Use animated expressions when this happens. As children build their structures, talk to them about how they can problem solve by adding support and stability to the structure by starting with a wide base. Comment on the height of the tower and count the blocks with them. Encourage cooperative play as children build their structure. This activity is ideal for both indoor and outdoor environments.

Hint: If a child intentionally knocks down another child's structure, use this teachable moment to talk about the importance of respecting everyone's work. You can start older infants on building using soft cloth-covered foam blocks.

Expand the Activity

• Add cars and trucks to the play experience.

• Use cardboard boxes and recycled materials for the building activity.

• Demonstrate how children can engineer bridges and incline planes to add to the building experience.

Build Vocabulary

blocks, stack, build, engineer, count, move, leverage, stable, high, low, tall, short, wide, height, base, tumble, side by side, bridge, incline plane

Inquiry Questions and Comments

- Stacking blocks is fun. Look how high you built it. Oops! It fell down.

- If you want to build a really tall building, you need to start with a wide base. Let me show you how to do it. I put three blocks side by side. Now, you can stack on top of them. Way to go!

- How high should we make it?

- Tell me about what you are building.

- What if you add another block? Let's see what happens.

Home-School Connection

Children can use household items, such as plastic storage containers, to build a structure.

Suggested Books

- *First 100 Words (Bright Baby)* by Roger Priddy

- *Goodnight, Goodnight, Construction Site* by Sherri Duskey Rinker

- *Look at That Building* by Scot Ritchie

- *One Big Building: A Counting Book about Construction* by Michael Dahl and Todd Ouren

- *Richard Scarry's Best First Book Ever!* by Richard Scarry

- *Roadwork* by Sally Sutton

- *Roar! A Noisy Counting Book* by Pamela Duncan Edwards and Henry Cole

- *Tap Tap Bang Bang* by Emma Garcia

- *Tip Tip Dig Dig* by Emma Garcia

- *Toot Toot Beep Beep* by Emma Garcia

Circle Balance

Ages

○ **Infants**

○ **Toddlers**

● **Twos**

STEM Concepts

● **Science** (Physical science)

○ **Technology**

● **Engineering** (Engineering)

● **Math** (Number sense and operations, Shapes, Spatial relationships)

Learning Outcomes

Children experiment with balance and weight as they learn how to keep the items from falling off the top of the cardboard circle. They will learn how to add and remove items in order to create balance on the cardboard ball. Children will gain experience with how to keep something upright and balanced.

Teaching Tips

A balance will remain steady and upright based on the weight of each object and the distribution of objects placed on its surface. Weight is how heavy or light something is. The balance will tilt to one side or the other depending on which objects are heavier or lighter in weight. By adjusting or removing objects, you can distribute the weight more evenly, causing the scale to remain steady and upright.

Materials

• 10–12-inch cardboard circle

• 3–4-inch Styrofoam ball

• serrated knife

• glue gun

• items for balancing, such as counting bears, rocks, seashells, plastic cars, or animals

Getting Ready

Cut the Styrofoam ball in half. You will use only half of the Styrofoam ball for the balance. Using a glue gun, glue the middle of the cardboard circle to the flat side of the Styrofoam ball. Once the glue has cooled, flatten the bottom of the Styrofoam ball slightly by cutting off the bottom ⅛ inch with the knife. This will keep the ball more upright for the balancing activity.

How To

Let the children examine the circle and Styrofoam balance before you begin. Explain how to place or remove items on the cardboard circle to keep the circle in balance. Model how to adjust items to help maintain the circle in balance.

Hint: Trimming the bottom of the Styrofoam ball will help the cardboard circle stay upright. If you don't trim the bottom, it will tip over very easily and may be frustrating for young children. If you cut too much off the bottom of the ball, use the serrated knife to trim it round again. Be sure to closely supervise young children to make sure they don't place small objects in their mouths.

Expand the Activity

- Have the children make predictions about which items they can use to keep the cardboard circle upright.

- Have the children count how many items they are able to stack on top of the cardboard circle before the items fall off.

Build Vocabulary

balance, stabilize, tilt, upright, fall, move, adjust, circle, Styrofoam, add, shift, take away

Inquiry Questions and Comments

- Let's look at the balance. What shape is this? Yes, it's a circle.

- The cardboard piece is flat and the Styrofoam piece has a round bottom.

- We're going see how many items we can place on the cardboard circle before it tips over.

- Which items should we use?

- What's your prediction about how many it will take to keep the balance upright?

- Let's count the items.

Home-School Connection

Invite parents to talk to their children about objects that are heavy and light. If they have a kitchen scale or bathroom scale, they could weigh the items. Encourage parents to ask children to predict which household items are heavy or light.

Suggested Books

- *Barnyard Dance* by Sandra Boynton

- *Dancing Feet* by Lindsey Craig

- *From Head to Toe* (board book) by Eric Carle

- *My First Body* by DK Publishing

Color, Count, and Sort

Ages

○ Infants
● Toddlers
● Twos

STEM Concepts

○ Science
○ Technology
○ Engineering
● Math (Number sense and operations, Patterns and classification, Spatial relationships, Mathematical reasoning)

Learning Outcomes

Children will gain experience with number sense and operations, including counting, sorting, and one-to-one correspondence.

Teaching Tips

Number sense and operations is developed as children count and sort the craft sticks. Children will also learn to identify the name of colors as they place the colored craft sticks in the matching slots.

Materials

- medium-size box with a lid, such as a shoebox
- white construction paper or contact paper
- scissors
- tape
- box cutter
- colored markers
- colored craft sticks

Getting Ready

Cover the top of the box with white paper. Using a box cutter, cut four slots in the top of the box. Using a colored marker, color the edges of each slit either red, yellow, blue, or green. For example, color one of the slots red for a red craft stick.

How To

Invite the children to sort the craft sticks first, then demonstrate how they can slide them into the slots. Count the sticks with the children as they place them in the slots.

Hint: Wider slots will be easier for children to use, so cut the slots wide enough for the children to easily slide the craft sticks through them.

Expand the Activity

- Cut pieces of colored construction paper into 5-inch squares and write the name of the color on the paper. Place the colored papers around the classroom. Give each child a colored craft stick and have the children go on a hunt around the room to look for the colored square that matches their stick.

- Give each child a colored craft stick and have them pair up with a child who has the same colored stick. Gather the sticks and repeat the activity, giving each child a different colored stick.

Build Vocabulary

craft stick, match, sort, same, different, slide, slot, names of colors

Inquiry Questions and Comments

- Watch me as I slide the craft stick into the slot. Now, it's your turn.

- Let's sort all of the craft sticks by color. We can put the red ones here and the blue ones there.

- Let's look at this box.

- What do you see on the top? Those are called slots. We're going to slide the sticks into the slots.

- What color do you see on the slot? Red, that's correct!

- Okay, let's put all of our red sticks in here.

- Let's count as you slide the sticks into the slot: 1, 2, 3 . . .

- How many sticks did you slide into the box?

Home-School Connection

Invite parents to go on a color hunt around their house with their child. They can select one item such as a red sock and ask their child to find other things that are the color red. Then, they can move on to another color.

Suggested Books

- *Baby Touch and Feel: Colors and Shapes* by DK Publishing

- *Baby Touch and Feel: Numbers* by DK Publishing

- *Bright Baby Colors, ABC, and Numbers* by Roger Priddy

- *First 100 Numbers Colors Shapes (Bright Baby)* by Roger Priddy

- *Mouse Paint* by Ellen Stoll Walsh

- *My Crayons Talk* by Patricia Hubbard

- *My Very First Book of Numbers* by Eric Carle

- *White Rabbit's Color Book* by Alan Baker

Cotton Swab Painting

Ages

○ **Infants**
● **Toddlers**
● **Twos**

STEM Concepts

● **Science** (Physical science)
○ **Technology**
○ **Engineering**
● **Math** (Number sense and operations)

Learning Outcomes

Children will gain an understanding of how colors can be mixed together to create new colors, one-to-one correspondence, and number sense.

Teaching Tips

The primary colors of red, yellow, and blue can be mixed together to create the secondary colors of purple, orange, and green. Combine red and blue to make purple. Yellow and red makes orange, and blue and yellow makes green.

Materials

• white paper
• muffin tin
• red, yellow, and blue liquid watercolor paint
• cotton swabs
• painting aprons

• 2 or 3 plastic bowls of water to rinse out the cotton swabs or add more water to the paint
• paper towels for cleanup

Getting Ready

No additional preparation is needed.

How To

Give each child a piece of white paper. Place red, blue, and yellow liquid watercolor paint in separate muffin tin cups. Place a cotton swab in each of the colors. Model for the children how they can paint using the cotton swab. You can model how to make dots, swirls, and lines on the paper. Talk to the children about the colors they are using and what colors they are making.

Hint: Have lots of cotton swabs available, as the children will need new ones to use in their painting. Adding drops of water to the paper can change the experience.

Expand the Activity

• Add a second muffin tin with secondary paint colors (purple, green, and orange) and invite the children to paint and mix the colors together.

• Add white and black liquid watercolor paint in containers to add to the painting experience.

• Place an unused piece of paper on top of each of the children's paintings. Have the children press down on the paper and then lift it up to create a monoprint. Talk to the children about what they see on both pieces of paper.

Build Vocabulary

cotton swab, watercolor paint, paper, red, yellow, blue, colors, dots, swirls, lines, together

Inquiry Questions and Comments

- What colors do you see in the muffin tins? Yes, you're correct. We have three colors: red, yellow, and blue.

- When you mix colors together, you can make new colors.

- What happened when you mixed the red and yellow paint together?

- What color did it make? Yes, you made orange!

- What new colors do you think you can make when we mix the colors together?

- What do you see?

- What do you think will happen if we mix another color on the paper?

Home-School Connection

Invite parents to repeat the activity at home using a watercolor paint set or by adding a few drops of food coloring into small containers of water. Invite children to paint on paper or paper towels using a cotton swab. Talk to the children about the colors they are using and making.

Suggested Books

- *Bright Baby Colors, ABC, and Numbers* by Roger Priddy

- *First 100 Numbers Colors Shapes (Bright Baby)* by Roger Priddy

- *Mouse Paint* by Ellen Stoll Walsh

- *White Rabbit's Color Book* by Alan Baker

Drip, Drop, Drip, Drop

Ages

○ **Infants**
● **Toddlers**
● **Twos**

STEM Concepts

● **Science** (Physical science, Earth science)
● **Technology** (Simple tools)
○ **Engineering**
○ **Math**

Learning Outcomes

Children will gain an understanding of absorption as they drop water onto objects.

Teaching Tips

Absorption is the process by which one substance takes up another substance, or is absorbed.

Materials

· 4 kitchen sponges

· scissors

· plastic tray deep enough to hold the wet sponges

· paper towels

· eyedroppers

· small squeeze bottles

· small cups

· bowl of water

Getting Ready

Cut each of the sponges in half with scissors.

How To

Have the children touch the dry paper towel and dry sponges and discuss how they feel. Set a dry paper towel and dry sponge aside for later. Fill squeeze bottles and small cups with water. Model how to use the eyedroppers and squeeze bottles for the children. Show them how they can drop water from the eyedroppers and squeeze bottles onto a paper towel or sponge. Encourage them to use the eyedroppers or squeeze bottles to drop the water onto a paper towel or sponge. Have them touch the wet paper towel and the sponge. Then, have the children touch the dry ones and compare the differences between them.

Hint: Use regular kitchen sponges, not sponges with abrasive sides.

Expand the Activity

· Take the children outside and have them use watering cans or buckets of water to pour water onto a potted plant or the soil. Come back later and discuss how the soil has absorbed the water.

· Fill two separate bowls with water tinted with two different shades of food coloring. Encourage the children to use the eyedroppers to drop one color onto another on the paper towel and observe how the colors blend together.

Build Vocabulary

sponge, squeeze bottle, wet, dry, eyedropper, absorb, drop

Inquiry Questions and Comments

- Let's feel the sponge. What does it feel like to you?

- What do you think will happen when we add water to the sponge?

- Let's squeeze the sponge. What's happening?

Home-School Connection

Invite parents to point out things that absorb at home, such as how the sponge gets wet when washing dishes or how the washcloth absorbs water in the bathtub. Invite children to engage in this process too.

Suggested Books

- *Baby Touch and Feel: Splish! Splash!* by DK Publishing

- *Five Little Ducks* by Annie Kubler and Penny Ives

- *My Five Senses* by Aliki

- *My Five Senses* by Margaret Miller

- *Sally in the Sand* by Stephen Huneck

- *Richard Scarry's Best First Book Ever!* by Richard Scarry

- *What Makes the Seasons?* by Megan Montague Cash

Explore the Weather

Ages

○ **Infants**

○ **Toddlers**

● **Twos**

STEM Concepts

● **Science** (Physical science, Life science, Earth science)

○ **Technology**

○ **Engineering**

○ **Math**

Learning Outcomes

Children will gain knowledge on physical, life, and earth science as they learn about the four seasons.

Teaching Tips

Children begin to notice the effects of the weather and seasonal changes in their daily lives.

Materials

Books about the earth and the four seasons and photos of the sun, rain, snow, clouds, wind, and rainbows.

Getting Ready

No additional preparation is needed.

How To

Show children photos and describe natural objects in the sky such as the sun, rain, snow, clouds, wind, and rainbows. Explain wind, air, rain, and snow and how they are all part of the weather. Connect the weather to how living things need rain and sun to grow. Explain how the weather changes during the four seasons. Explain the season you are currently in. Explain what the weather is like outside. As you go for walks or play outdoors, explain the weather you see. Document the weather by taking pictures and posting them so children can see the changes in the weather around them.

Hint: Children often connect the weather with the clothes they wear and what activities they do in different seasons. For example, they will wear warm coats, gloves, and boots in the winter to stay warm.

Expand the Activity

• Explain how the light from the sun leaves a silhouette or shadow of an object. Walk outdoors and point out shadows to the children.

• Take a prism outdoors or place it on a windowsill. Point out that when the sunlight shines through the prism, it produces rainbow colors. Explain why we see rainbows, show the children an actual rainbow, or show a picture of one. Talk about the colors of the rainbow.

• In a sunny place on the sidewalk, place a large piece of butcher paper. Draw each child's shadow on the paper. Let the children color their shadow and take it home.

Build Vocabulary

weather, seasons, fall, winter, spring, summer, sun, moon, stars, rain, snow, clouds, wind, rainbow, colors, prisms, shadows, light

Inquiry Questions and Comments

- It's raining outside today. What does the sky look like when it rains?

- If the sun comes out while it's still raining, we might get to see a rainbow.

- What does it feel like when it snows? Is it cold or hot outside?

- What clothes do we wear if it's cold and snowy outside?

- Why do we wear these clothes?

Home-School Connection

Invite parents to talk about the natural objects they see, such as the sky and clouds. Encourage them to talk about the moon and stars that are seen at night.

Suggested Books

- *Planting a Rainbow* by Lois Ehlert

- *What Is the Weather Today?* by Rebecca Bondor

- *What Makes the Seasons?* by Megan Montague Cash

- *White Rabbit's Color Book* by Alan Baker

- *The Wind Blew* by Pat Hutchins

- *A Windy Day in Spring* by Charles Ghigna and Laura Watson

Exploring Light

Ages

○ **Infants**

○ **Toddlers**

● **Twos**

STEM Concepts

● **Science** (Physical science, Life science, Earth science,)

● **Technology** (Simple tools)

○ **Engineering**

● **Math** (Number sense and operations, Patterns and classification, Shapes and relationships, Measurement)

Learning Outcomes

Children will deepen their understanding of light, density, and transparency as they explore and investigate materials using a light table. Children will explore the properties and characteristics of different materials.

Teaching Tips

Light tables provide children with opportunities to increase their fine-motor skills as they explore and investigate. An object is transparent when light is transmitted or projected through it. Objects are made up of varying degrees of density and transparency. Light tables can be used to develop all areas of STEM.

Materials

• light table

• variety of materials that have different degrees of transparency, such as rocks, buttons, sand, seashells, alphabet and number magnets, buttons, tissue paper, feathers, pieces of wood, keys, leaves, paint, and playdough

• basket for collecting items

• magnifying glasses

Getting Ready

• Place the light table against a wall or in a corner away from natural light.

• Gather items for viewing and place them in baskets near the light table. Items may be completely open-ended or selected to support a classroom theme.

How To

Help children collect additional objects from the classroom or playground and place in a basket. Talk to them about how each item looks and feels and make predictions about whether the light will shine through the items. Encourage children to select dense items, such as play-dough, rocks, sea shells, or pieces of wood. Invite the children to place these items on the light table and examine how they look with the light underneath them. Next, have children examine other items that are more transparent, such as tissue paper or clear plastic. Help the children identify which items they can see light through and which ones they can't. Encourage children to explore counting, sorting, and classifying the items on top of the light table. Invite children to examine the items in more detail by using a magnifying glass.

Hint: If you don't have a light table, there are lots of instructions online for how to make one using an under-the-bed storage bin with a clear top and white holiday lights. Be sure to closely supervise young children to make sure they don't place small objects in their mouths.

Expand the Activity

Place a mirror against the edge of the light table for children to see the reflection of what they are exploring. Provide materials such as small wood blocks for children to build a structure on top of the light table. Place a sensory bottle (see page 130) on top of the table and see how the light shines through it.

Build Vocabulary

light table, clear, dense, solid, plastic, wood, letters, numbers, rocks, feathers, buttons

Inquiry Questions and Comments

- What are the materials you're using?

- What do you see when you look at the rocks and seashells?

- What happens when you place one rock on top of another?

- Can you see the light through any of the rocks?

- What objects can you see light through?

Home-School Connection

Invite parents to make a light table following directions found on the Internet. They can collect items from home and discuss transparency. Place the items on top of a mirror and show the child the reflection. Encourage the child to draw a picture of their play experience.

Suggested Books

- *Baby Touch and Feel: Numbers* by DK Publishing

- *Bright Baby Colors, ABC, and Numbers First Words* by Roger Priddy

- *Brown Rabbit's Shape Book* by Alan Baker

- *First 100 Numbers Colors Shapes (Bright Baby)* by Roger Priddy

- *My Five Senses* by Aliki

- *My Five Senses* by Margaret Miller

- *White Rabbit's Color Book* by Alan Baker

Fast Flyers

Ages

○ **Infants**

○ **Toddlers**

● **Twos**

STEM Concepts

● **Science** (Physical science)

● **Technology** (Technology, Simple machine and simple tools)

● **Engineering** (Engineering)

● **Math** (Measurement)

Learning Outcomes

Children will help engineer the cording and weights to create this motion activity. They will gain a sense of gravity and motion.

Teaching Tips

Gravity is the natural force that tends to cause physical objects to move toward each other and causes objects to fall toward Earth. Heavier objects will drop faster down the rope when there is more tension on the cord. The slope of an incline plane will increase or decrease the speed of a falling object.

Materials

• heavy cording or heavy yarn

• scissors

• a heavy object with a hole in it, such as a washer or a magnet with a hole in the center

that is large enough for the cord or yarn to easily slide through

• a door handle or knob attached to a door

Getting Ready

Cut the cording to 3–5 feet in length. Take the object that will slide, or "fly" down the cord and test it out at home. If it doesn't fly easily, add a magnet piece to it or find a heavier object for flying.

How To

Secure the cording on a door handle or doorknob. Slide the cording through the center of the object and move the flying object to the top of the cording. Let children hold the piece in place while you tighten the cording near the floor. Be sure the object is heavy enough to easily slide or zip down the cording. Have the child let go of the object and watch it go flying.

Hint: Heavier objects will slide down faster. A greater incline will increase the speed of the motion. You can use a large Lego piece for this activity. Assemble it so that there is a hole at the top for the cord to slide through. Be sure to closely supervise young children to make sure they don't place small objects in their mouths.

Expand the Activity

• Try using a different kind of cording or yarn to see how the activity differs.

• Set up two cords of different lengths. Using a second washer of equal weight, release the washers at the same time and watch them race down the cording. Ask the children to predict which one will be fastest—the one with the shorter cord or the longer cord.

Build Vocabulary

build, engineer, tie, pull, slip, tight, gravity, incline, motion, distance, tension, measurement

Inquiry Questions and Comments

- Let's feel the washer. What does it feel like?

- Let's tie one end of the cord to the door handle. Let's slip the cord through the hole in the washer.

- You hold the washer tight and then let it go when I say, "Go!"

- You can hold the other end of the cording on the floor nice and tight. We can all watch as gravity works to pull the washer down.

- What do you think will happen if the cord isn't tight? Will the washer go faster or slower?

- What will happen if we raise it up higher?

- What other objects should we explore? We need to find objects that have holes in them. Let's try this one. What do you predict will happen?

Home-School Connection

Parents can replicate this activity at home using household items such as canning rings, bracelets, or small stacking rings.

Suggested Books

- *National Geographic Little Kids First Big Book of Why* by Catherine Hughes

- *Richard Scarry's A Day at the Airport* by Richard Scarry

- *Richard Scarry's Best First Book Ever!* by Richard Scarry

- *Rosie Revere, Engineer* by Andrea Beaty

Flower Bracelets

Ages

○ **Infants**

● **Toddlers**

● **Twos**

STEM Concepts

● **Science** (Life science, Earth science)

○ **Technology**

● **Engineering** (Engineering)

● **Math** (Number sense and operations, Classification, Measurement)

Learning Outcomes

Children will explore and gain a respect for the outdoor environment and an awareness of living things, such as plants and flowers. They will explore elements of both life science and earth science.

Teaching Tips

Children can learn about life and earth science through nature walks and exploration. Help children differentiate between living and nonliving things and explain the life cycle of trees, plants, and flowers.

Materials

• masking tape

• scissors

• items found on a nature walk for decorating the bracelet

Getting Ready

No additional preparation is needed.

How To

Measure and cut a piece of masking tape to fit loosely around a toddler's wrist. Tape the ends together, sticky side out. Go for a walk outdoors and invite the children to pick up fallen flowers or leaves and place them on the sticky side of the tape. Ask them to smell the flowers and leaves that they found. Ask them to describe what they see and smell. Remind them not to put any of the flowers or leaves in their mouths.

Hint: If you are working with infants, you may want to put the tape on your own wrist, so they can see what you've collected. Be sure to closely supervise young children to make sure they don't place small objects in their mouths.

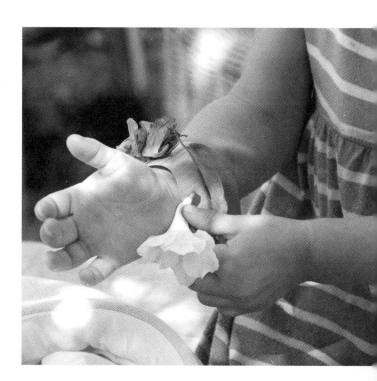

Expand the Activity

Bring two or three different kinds of flowers to class and let the children examine them. They can smell them, feel them, and examine their petals using a magnifying glass. Place the flowers in a vase and set them on a table.

Build Vocabulary

masking tape, sticky, secure, wrist, place, flower petals, leaves, smell

Inquiry Questions and Comments

- We're going to go on a nature walk to look at plants and flowers. We want to respect and care for nature. Let me know if you see a flower or a leaf on the ground.

- What color is the flower?

- What does it smell like?

- Here's another one. How does it look different from the other one?

- Touch the leaf. How does the leaf feel?

Home-School Connection

Invite parents to take their child for a walk around the neighborhood. Encourage them to point out the plants and flowers they see. Suggest they visit a nearby arboretum or public garden.

Suggested Books

- *Are You a Bee?* by Judy Allen
- *Are You a Butterfly?* by Judy Allen
- *Are You a Ladybug?* by Judy Allen
- *Bugs* by Andrews McMeel
- *Bugs! Bugs! Bugs!* by Bob Barner
- *Counting in the Garden* by Kim Parker
- *I Love Bugs* by Philemon Sturges
- *In the Tall, Tall Grass* by Denise Fleming
- *Planting a Rainbow* by Lois Ehlert
- *The Surprise Garden* by Zoe Hall

Fresh from the Farm

Ages

○ Infants

○ Toddlers

● Twos

STEM Concepts

● **Science** (Life Science, Earth science)

● **Technology** (Simple tools)

○ **Engineering**

● **Math** (Classification)

Learning Outcomes

Children will gain knowledge of what fruits and vegetables grow on a farm and the important role the environment plays in helping crops grow.

Teaching Tips

Farms can produce a variety of crops, including fruits and vegetables. Crops need air, water, and soil to grow.

Materials

• books about farms and crops

• variety of fruits and vegetables

• knives

• cutting board

• paper plates

• napkins

Getting Ready

Read and discuss books about what grows on a farm. On the day of the activity, pre-cut some fruit and vegetables for children to taste. Be sure and leave at least one fruit and vegetable uncut so the children can taste them in their whole state.

How To

Introduce the different fruits and vegetables to the children. Let them investigate a whole piece of fruit or vegetable. Explain the different parts of the fruit or vegetable, such as the seeds, stem, or skin. Introduce fruits and vegetables separately, placing a cut piece of fruit or vegetable on the child's plate and letting them explore and taste it. Talk to the children about different fruits and vegetables and what they need to grow.

Warning: Be aware of any food allergies the children may have and eliminate those fruits and vegetables from the activity.

Expand the Activity

- Sort the fruits and vegetables by color.

- Select one whole fruit or vegetable and let the child draw it.

- Make a smoothie with different kinds of fruit and let the children have it as a snack.

Build Vocabulary

see, taste, smell, touch, fruit, vegetable, grow, soil, air, sun, seed, stem

Inquiry Questions and Comments

- Fruits and vegetables grow on a farm. We are going to explore some fruits and vegetables today and see how they taste.

- Here is a . . . What color is it? How does it taste?

- Which fruit or vegetable did you like best? Why?

Home-School Connection

Invite parents to go to their local supermarket. As they walk through the produce section, they can identify different fruits and vegetables with their child.

Suggested Books

- *Apples and Pumpkins* by Anne Rockwell

- *Baby Touch and Feel: Farm* by DK Publishing

- *Big Red Barn* by Margaret Wise Brown

- *Food from Farms* by Nancy Dickmann

- *Eating the Alphabet: Fruits and Vegetables from A to Z* by Lois Ehlert

- *From the Garden: A Counting Book about Growing Food* by Michael Dahl and Todd Ouren

- *How Are You Peeling?* by Saxton Freymann

- *The Little Gardener* by Jan Gerardi

- *My Five Senses* by Aliki

- *My Five Senses* by Margaret Miller

- *My Very First Book of Food* by Eric Carle

- *Planting a Rainbow* by Lois Ehlert

Garden Herbs

Ages

○ **Infants**

○ **Toddlers**

● **Twos**

STEM Concepts

● **Science** (Life Science, Earth Science)

● **Technology** (Simple tools)

○ **Engineering**

● **Math** (Patterns and classification)

Learning Outcomes

Children will explore with their senses a variety of culinary herbs.

Teaching Tips

Most culinary herbs can be dried or used fresh in cooking. Each herb has its own unique characteristics, including how it looks, smells, and tastes.

Materials

• fresh culinary herbs, such as basil, rosemary, mint, cilantro, parsley, and oregano

• tray or baking sheet

• paper towels

• magnifying glasses

Getting Ready

Purchase or pick from your garden a variety of culinary herbs, such as fresh basil, rosemary, mint, cilantro, parsley, and oregano.

How To

Place paper towels on the tray or baking sheet and place the herbs on it. Introduce herbs to the children one at a time. Let them look, smell, and taste the individual herbs. Share with the children about both life and earth science, explaining how herbs need water, sunlight, soil, and nutrients to grow. Let the children investigate the herbs on the trays. Document how they describe the herbs.

Hint: Try to pick as much of the herb as possible so children can see all parts of the plant, including the leaves, stem, and roots if possible. Some herbs have a stronger taste and smell than others. Don't pressure children to taste or smell an herb if they find it offensive. By placing the herbs on a tray, children can explore at their leisure.

Expand the Activity

• Purchase small herb plants at the local nursery and plant an herb garden with the children.

• Crush herbs with a mortar and pestle and let the children explore and examine the herbs in a different state.

• Bring dried herbs from home and talk about the drying process. Have children compare and contrast fresh and dried herbs.

• Make a vegetable dip using a few of the herbs and let the children taste the dip.

Build Vocabulary

herbs, fresh, basil, rosemary, mint, cilantro, parsley, oregano, grow, nature, cut, pick, dry

Inquiry Questions and Comments

- The herbs grow in the garden. Each of these herbs has a different kind of leaf, smell, and taste.

- What do you see when you look at this piece of mint?

- What do the leaves look like? Are the edges of the leaves smooth or jagged?

- How does the mint leaf look different than the rosemary leaves?

- Which one do you like best? Why?

- Which herbs do you like to smell?

Home-School Connection

Invite parents to talk about the herbs they use in cooking. Encourage the children to help add the herbs to favorite family recipes.

Suggested Books

- *Counting in the Garden* by Kim Parker

- *Eating the Alphabet: Fruits and Vegetables from A to Z* by Lois Ehlert

- *Food from Farms* by Nancy Dickmann

- *From the Garden: A Counting Book about Growing Food* by Michael Dahl and Todd Ouren

- *The Little Gardener* by Jan Gerardi

- *My Five Senses* by Aliki

- *My Five Senses* by Margaret Miller

- *Quick as a Cricket* by Audrey Wood and Don Wood

Here We Go

Ages

- ● **Infants**
- ● **Toddlers**
- ○ **Twos**

STEM Concepts

- ● **Science** (Physical science)
- ● **Technology** (Simple machines)
- ○ **Engineering**
- ● **Math** (Number sense and operations, Spatial relationships, Mathematical reasoning)

Learning Outcomes

Children will gain a sense of the properties of physical science and simple machines, such as the push and pull of a cart or wheeled toy. They will gain number sense and operations as they place items inside the cart and then remove them.

Teaching Tips

Children learn about balance and motion as they use a push and pull toy to stabilize their walking. They learn about one-to-one correspondence as they place items in a container. Children begin to understand the simple machine of a wheel and axle as they spin the wheel of a push and pull toy.

Materials

- Select a variety of push and pull toys, such as trucks, cars, planes, balls, buggies, wagons, and shopping carts. Toys should have a basket or container large enough to carry items.
- Toys and items to place in the push and pull toys, such as small balls, soft plush toys, dolls, cars, trucks, plastic animals

Getting Ready

No additional preparation is needed.

How To

Provide children with a variety of large and small push and pull toys. Identify the name and parts of each toy. Model for young children how to place items inside the toy. Count the toy items

as children place them in the cart. Choose toys that can be used in both indoor and outdoor areas. Include large, sturdy push and pull toys that can help stabilize children who are learning to walk and stand on their own.

Expand the Activity

Set small toys, such as cars, trucks, and balls in baskets or containers that are easily accessible for play in all the learning centers, both inside and outside. Model how children can incorporate these toys with other play materials. For example, you could help the children build ramps out of blocks and show them how they can roll and push the cars down the ramp.

Build Vocabulary

push, pull, over, under, carry, move, trucks, cars, shopping cart, wagon, buggy

Inquiry Questions and Comments

- Look at you walking! You can push the cart around the room.

- What toys should we put in the cart? I'm going to count them. One, two, three cars.

- Can you put the cars in the cart and take them to the block area?

- If we turn the cart on its side, you can see the wheels moving around.

- Let me show you how to spin the wheels. Now you try!

Home-School Connection

Share with parents the importance of providing children with push and pull toys that will help develop walking skills. Encourage them to provide children with opportunities to fill containers and baskets with favorite toys.

Suggested Books

- *Baby Touch and Feel: Trucks* by DK Publishing

- *Big Book of Things That Go* by DK Publishing

- *Big and Little: Things That Go* by Rebecca Bondor

- *Dig Dig Digging* by Margaret Mayo

- *First 100 Trucks (Bright Baby)* by Roger Priddy

- *Let's Count Trucks: A Fun Kids' Counting Book for Toddler Boys and Children Age 2 to 5* by Alina Niemi

- *Little Blue Truck* by Alice Schertle

- *Little Blue Truck Leads the Way* by Alice Schertle

- *My Truck Is Stuck* by Kevin Lewis

- *Richard Scarry's Best First Book Ever!* by Richard Scarry

Hole in One

Ages

● **Infants**

● **Toddlers**

○ Twos

STEM Concepts

● **Science** (Physical science)

○ **Technology**

○ **Engineering**

● **Math** (Mathematics, Number sense and operations, Shapes and spatial relationships, Mathematical reasoning)

Learning Outcomes

Children will experience understanding of number sense, operations, cause and effect, and one-to-one correspondence by playing with a pegboard or a stacking ring.

Teaching Tips

Children need experience playing with objects that can be counted and sorted while learning number sense, operations, cause and effect, and one-to-one correspondence.

Materials

• large stacking rings

• pegboards

• sorting cubes or buckets

Getting Ready

No additional preparation is needed.

How To

Place either stacking rings or a pegboard in front of each child, along with some sorting cubes or buckets. Model how to place the rings on their post, the pegs in the pegboard, and rings and pegs into the sorting cubes or buckets. Talk about how there is a hole or space in the toy where the items are to be placed. At this age, the task for young children is to just explore how to place the rings, insert the pegs, or place the items into the sorting cube. Identify the colors and shapes being used, but don't expect young children to get them in the correct order.

Hint: Offer one toy at a time. Children will just be exploring the materials and gaining a sense of where to place items on the pegboard or stacking ring.

Expand the Activity

• Help the child sort items by color or shape. Count the pegs or rings as the child engages in the activity.

• Separate the items by colors or shapes. Focus on one color at a time, and have the child identify another object that is the same color. In this modification, just introduce the concept of different colors, but don't expect the child to understand color differentiation.

Build Vocabulary

pegs, rings, board, hole, place, stack, in, out, round, turn, twist

Inquiry Questions and Comments

- This is called a pegboard. There are holes in the board for each peg. Can you see the hole? Touch the peg and run your finger through the hole on the pegboard.

- Watch as I place the peg in a hole on the board. One peg goes in each hole.

- Will you try with me?

- Look how we can stack one peg on top of another one.

Home-School Connection

Invite parents to select ten to twelve household items of several colors. Place the items in front of the child. Older infants will just play and explore the items. Toddlers will begin to sort like objects. Model how you count objects by touching each object.

Suggested Books

- *Baby Touch and Feel: Colors and Shapes* by DK Publishing

- *Baby Touch and Feel: Numbers* by DK Publishing

- *Bright Baby Colors, ABC, and Numbers First Words* by Roger Priddy

- *Brown Rabbit's Shape Book* by Alan Baker

- *First 100 Numbers Colors Shapes (Bright Baby)* by Roger Priddy

- *Roar! A Noisy Counting Book* by Pamela Duncan Edwards and Henry Cole

Ice Cold Mountains

Ages

○ **Infants**

○ **Toddlers**

● **Twos**

STEM Concepts

● **Science** (Physical science, Life science, Earth science)

● **Technology** (Simple tools)

● **Engineering** (Engineering)

● **Math** (Number sense, Measurement, Mathematical reasoning)

Learning Outcomes

Children will build an ice "mountain" as they are introduced to the properties of water. They will also experience what happens when you sprinkle salt on top of ice.

Teaching Tips

Salt lowers the freezing point of water, forcing the ice to melt briefly and then refreeze. It's important to note that salt alone can't melt ice. It must first be combined with water to start the melting process.

Materials

• water

• variety of containers in which to freeze water, such as ice cube trays, gelatin molds, muffin tins, plastic storage boxes

• pictures of mountains

• camera

• small toys for freezing

• bowls of water

• salt

• several large buckets

• items for pouring water such as funnels, sponges, plastic cups, turkey basters

Getting Ready

Collect all the containers for freezing water and make space in the freezer for containers.

How To

Day 1: Show children pictures of mountains, and explain that you are going to build an ice mountain. Set out the empty containers that you plan to fill with water, and ask the child to sort and count them. Using the empty containers, assist the children in creating a plan or model

for building their mountain. Take photos to document the model. You will need this for the construction on day 2. Talk about the properties of water, and discuss the children's prediction on what will happen when the water freezes. Place the toy items in ice cube trays, gelatin molds, or ice molds, fill with water, and freeze overnight.

Day 2: Review the plan created the day before with the children. Unmold the frozen water into several buckets. Sprinkle salt directly on the ice in the buckets and let the children build mountains of ice. Let the children use the items for pouring to add additional water to help the ice melt, and let them play in the water. After all the ice has melted, collect and sort all the small toys and count them. Document the building process.

Hint: Have a bucket of warm water handy in case little hands get too cold. Be sure to closely supervise young children to make sure they don't place small objects in their mouths.

Expand the Activity

Instead of adding objects to the water, add different colors of food coloring to the water. Children can make predictions about which color of ice will melt first and then build a colorful mountain. You can also add paper towels underneath it to see what colors blend together after the ice has melted.

Build Vocabulary

water, freeze, ice, melt, salt, mountain, overnight, build, stack, sprinkle

Inquiry Questions and Comments

• How many items did you count?

• What do you think is going to happen to this item overnight in the water?

• What object do you want to freeze first? What container should we put it in?

• Do you think the object will sink or float? Why?

• Let's build a mountain with our ice. We can stack the pieces on top of each other like this.

• Let's see what happens to the ice when we sprinkle salt on it.

• What is happening?

• The ice is melting now.

• What is it becoming now? You're right! When the ice melts, it becomes water again!

Home-School Connection

Invite parents to conduct an ice experiment at home with their child where they take an ice cube and sprinkle salt on it to see how long it will take to melt.

Suggested Books

• *Baby Touch and Feel: Splish! Splash!* by DK Publishing

• *Baby Polar Bear* by Aubrey Lang and Wayne Lynch

• *My First Body* by DK Publishing

• *My Hands* by Aliki

• *National Geographic Little Kids First Big Book of Why* by Catherine Hughes

• *The Rainbow Fish* by Marcus Pfister and J. Alison James

• *Tacky the Penguin* by Helen Lester

Ice Fishing

Ages

○ **Infants**

● **Toddlers**

● **Twos**

STEM Concepts

● **Science** (Physical science, Life science, Earth science)

○ **Technology**

● **Engineering** (Engineering)

● **Math** (Number sense, Measurement, Mathematical reasoning)

Learning Outcomes

The children are going to experiment with ice and see what happens when you sprinkle salt on top of ice.

Teaching Tips

Salt lowers the freezing point and forces the ice to melt briefly before it refreezes. The string should cling to the ice cubes. It's important to note that salt alone can't melt ice. It must first be combined with water to start the melting process.

Materials

• 3 to 4 ice cubes

• small glass bowl

• room-temperature water

• salt

• 6–8-inch piece of string

• teaspoon

Getting Ready

Freeze water into ice cubes.

How To

Place the ice cubes in the small bowl of water. Be sure to allow an inch of empty space at the top of the bowl. The ice cubes will float to the top. Let the children feel the water before you add the ice cubes and after the ice has melted. Ask the children how the temperature of the water has changed. Document their responses.

Lay the piece of string across the top of the ice cubes. Pour about a teaspoon of salt in a child's hand. Have the child sprinkle the salt across the top of the ice cubes. Wait a minute or so. Have the child pull the string out and see what they catch!

Hint: The ice cubes should freeze again with the string attached. This is a great water displacement activity too.

Expand the Activity

• Freeze other liquids, such as milk or juice, to see if they will do the same thing.

• Make a graph to show how many children caught a specific number of ice cubes.

Build Vocabulary

ice, salt, melt, cold, freeze, cling, cube, float, string, catch

Inquiry Questions and Comments

- How does the water feel?

- What do you think will happen when we put the salt on the ice?

- Let's see what happens when you put the salt on the ice cubes. Let's put the string on top of the ice cubes.

- How did you catch the ice cube? The salt makes the ice cube melt and then the string clings to it.

- How many ice cubes do you think we will catch?

- Let's count how many ice cubes you caught.

Home-School Connection

Invite parents to re-create this experiment at home.

Suggested Books

- *Baby Touch and Feel: Splish! Splash!* by DK Publishing

- *Baby Polar Bear* by Aubrey Lang and Wayne Lynch

- *My First Body* by DK Publishing

- *My Hands* by Aliki

- *National Geographic Little Kids First Big Book of Why* by Catherine Hughes

- *The Rainbow Fish* by Marcus Pfister and J. Alison James

- *Tacky the Penguin* by Helen Lester

Leaf Prints

Ages

○ **Infants**

○ **Toddlers**

● **Twos**

STEM Concepts

● **Science** (Physical science, Life Science, Earth Science)

● **Technology** (Simple tools)

○ **Engineering**

● **Math** (Patterns and classification)

Learning Outcomes

Children will investigate and explore the parts of leaves while experiencing life science and the natural world.

Teaching Tips

Leaf rubbings give children a closer look at the structure of the leaf, including the stem, leaf, and veins. In most plants, the leaves provide food for the plant. The veins transport water, minerals, and food to the plant.

Materials

• variety of leaves

• magnifying glasses

• colored pencils

• crayons

• clipboards

• different kinds of paper, including wax paper, parchment paper, or tracing paper

• tape

Getting Ready

Go on a nature walk with the children and collect a variety of leaves for the rubbing activity.

How To

After collecting the leaves, let children investigate them using magnifying glasses. Show the children the different coloring materials. Place a leaf and paper on each clipboard, with the paper covering the leaf. The clipboard will help keep them in place as the child rubs the paper with the coloring materials. Let the children experiment with the rubbings by using different coloring materials and types of paper. Each paper's surface and the coloring tool will give a different kind of leaf rubbing experience. Tape the leaf rubbings to windows to allow light to

show through the paper. Tape the natural leaf up next to the leaf rubbing to show contrast.

Hint: Keep in mind that it's easy to tear the paper, so caution children who are using colored pencils not to press or rub too hard. Thinner paper will easily rip.

Expand the Activity

Use aluminum foil instead of paper. Place the foil on top of the leaf, and roll a pencil over the leaf. This will give you a raised print instead of a colored one.

Build Vocabulary

leaf, vein, stem, rub, pressure, crayon, pencil, paper

Inquiry Questions and Comments

- Where did we see the leaves? Yes, they were on the trees outside, and we picked the leaves that had fallen to the ground.

- How do the leaves look the same?

- How do the leaves look different from each other?

- How are the edges of the leaves different?

- What colors do you see in the leaves?

- This one is green and brown. What else do you see on the leaf?

- When you touch it, what does it feel like?

Home-School Connection

Invite parents to go for a nature walk with their children and collect leaves and flowers in their neighborhood. Invite the parents to place them in a basket for the children to explore and investigate.

Suggested Books

- *Autumn Leaves* by Ken Robbins

- *Awesome Autumn* by Bruce Goldstone

- *Counting in the Garden* by Kim Parker

- *First 100 Numbers Colors Shapes (Bright Baby)* by Roger Priddy

- *The Wind Blew* by Pat Hutchins

- *A Windy Day in Spring* by Charles Ghigna and Laura Watson

Let's Play Ball

Ages

- ● **Infants**
- ● **Toddlers**
- ○ **Twos**

STEM Concepts

- ● **Science** (Physical science)
- ● **Technology** (Simple machine)
- ○ **Engineering**
- ● **Math** (Number sense, Classification)

Learning Outcomes

Babies and toddlers are being introduced to the physical science property of motion as they roll and bounce balls. They are learning to classify the differences between objects as they play this activity.

Teaching Tips

Motion is a property of physical science. The motion and speed will vary with the weight, size, and surface tension or texture of various types of balls or objects.

Materials

Soft or rubber balls of various sizes. Select larger balls for younger children. Be sure the ball is large enough that the child cannot swallow or choke on it. Use smaller balls as the child gets older and develops more motor skills and dexterity.

Getting Ready

No additional preparation is needed.

How To

Sit on the floor with the child. Have your feet touching or almost touching the child's feet. With two hands roll the ball toward the child. Verbally describe what you are doing. Repeat the activity with the child rolling the ball toward you. Use different-sized balls for added learning opportunities.

Repeat the above activity with two or three children sitting in a circle with their feet touching. Ask the children to roll the ball to the child across from them. When they have mastered this task, add a second, smaller ball into the circle.

Expand the Activity

- Alternate between rolling and bouncing balls. You may need more space for this extended activity.

- Other objects such as small cars or trucks can be used for rolling. Model how to set up a small incline plane so they can see how balls and trucks can roll faster with an incline.

Build Vocabulary

balls, large, small, size, roll, bump, fast, slow, spin, twirl, pass, back and forth, around, between, next, take turns, touch, feet, share

Inquiry Questions and Comments

- We're going to roll the ball back and forth between us.

- Can you roll it back to me?

- Watch as the ball rolls and spins around.

- We are sharing the ball, as we pass the ball back and forth between us.

Home-School Connection

Have parents sit on the floor and roll a ball back and forth with the child.

Suggested Books

- *Rosie's Walk* by Pat Hutchins

- *My Hands* by Aliki

- *Where Is Baby's Beach Ball?* by Karen Katz

Let's Taste and See

Ages

○ **Infants**

○ **Toddlers**

● **Twos**

STEM Concepts

● **Science** (Life science, Earth science)

● **Technology** (Simple tools)

○ **Engineering**

● **Math** (Number sense and operations, Patterns and classification)

Learning Outcomes

Children will learn through their senses as they explore and investigate different kinds of fruits and vegetables.

Teaching Tips

Fruits and vegetables come in many types. Think of edible plants as having a fruit, a root, leaves, or a flower. Fruits and sometimes vegetables are the part of the plant that has seeds. Vegetables such as tomatoes or cucumbers are basically the fruit of the plant because they contain seeds. Spinach and lettuce are the leaves of the plants. Vegetables such as potatoes or carrots grow under the ground and are identified as the root of the plant. Cabbage, broccoli, and cauliflower, among other vegetables, are identified as the flower of a plant.

Materials

• fresh fruits and vegetables

• knife

• cutting board

• tray or baking sheet

• paper towels

• napkins or small paper plates

• magnifying glasses

Getting Ready

Purchase or pick from your garden a variety of fruits and vegetables for the children to examine and taste.

How To

Place paper towels on the tray or baking sheet. Introduce the fruits and vegetables to the children one at a time. Let them look, feel, and smell the individual fruits and vegetables before you cut them. You may want to introduce fruits separately from vegetables. Reserve some of the unhandled fruits and vegetables for sampling later. Talk to the children about where fruits and vegetables grow and that they need water, air, soil, and nutrients to grow. Describe the skin or peel of the fruits and vegetables. Cut the fruits and vegetables so children can see and feel the flesh or pulp. Point out the seeds of the fruits and vegetables and let the children examine them using the magnifying glasses. Document how they describe the different fruits and vegetables.

Hint: Some children may only want to see and touch the fruits and vegetables. Tasting the fruits and vegetables should be optional.

Warning: Be aware of any food allergies children might have and eliminate those fruits and vegetables from the activity.

Expand the Activity

• Cut up the fruit and make a smoothie out of them, using a blender. You can make a vegetable smoothie too, but adding apple juice as a natural sweetener is recommended.

• Place a variety of seeds on trays and let them air dry for a couple of days. Place the seeds on a large mirror and let the children examine, classify, count, and sort the dried seeds. By placing the seeds on a mirror, they will be able to examine both the front and back of the seeds.

Build Vocabulary

fruit, vegetables, knife, tray, cut, taste, smell, feel, seeds, pulp, flesh, colors

Inquiry Questions and Comments

• Let's look at the strawberries.

• Who's eaten a strawberry?

• What color is this strawberry?

• What do you see when you look at it with the magnifying glass? Yes, there are tiny seeds on it.

• What color is the tomato?

• What do you see when I cut it in half? Yes, there are seeds inside it.

• What color is the watermelon?

• Is it heavier or lighter than the strawberry?

Home-School Connection

Invite parents to point out different fruits and vegetables that the family eats at home or that they can find at the grocery store. Invite parents to introduce new fruits and vegetables to their children at home.

Suggested Books

• *The Apple Pie Tree* by Zoe Hall

• *Apples and Pumpkins* by Anne Rockwell

• *Baby Touch and Feel: Farm* by DK Publishing

• *Counting in the Garden* by Kim Parker

• *Eating the Alphabet: Fruits and Vegetables from A to Z* by Lois Ehlert

• *Food from Farms* by Nancy Dickmann

• *From the Garden: A Counting Book about Growing Food* by Michael Dahl and Todd Ouren

• *The Little Mouse, the Red Ripe Strawberry, and the Big Hungry Bear* by Audrey Wood and Don Wood

• *My Five Senses* by Aliki

• *My Five Senses* by Margaret Miller

Liquid Sensory Bottles

Ages

- ● Infants
- ● Toddlers
- ● Twos

STEM Concepts

- ● **Science** (Physical science)
- ● **Technology** (Simple tools)
- ○ **Engineering**
- ● **Math** (Engineering, Measurement)

Learning Outcomes

Children will examine the physical properties of motion while observing objects as they sink or float inside the bottle.

Teaching Tips

Sink and *float* are physical science concept words. Objects, including liquids, consist of atoms and molecules. Objects and liquids sink or float depending on the density, or mass or size, of their molecules. Water sinks because it is denser than oil.

Materials

- several clean, empty 16.9-ounce clear plastic water bottles
- water
- a few small rocks, toys, or heavy balls that can fit inside the water bottles
- vegetable oil
- food coloring
- funnel
- scissors
- colored duct tape
- dishwashing soap, optional

Getting Ready

Fill each bottle three-quarters full with water.

How To

Place the plastic bottle on a flat surface and set the funnel on top. Toddlers or younger children can take turns holding the bottle while you pour vegetable oil through the funnel. Toddlers and twos can help pour the vegetable oil into the funnel with assistance. Drop food coloring in the bottle and then drop the rocks or heavy balls into the bottle. Ask the children to watch as the items fall through the funnel into the bottle. Cut the colored duct tape and seal the top securely. Let the children examine and shake the sensory bottle.

Hint: If you wish to make a bubble sensory bottle, add 2 tablespoons of dishwashing soap. Be sure to closely supervise young children to make sure they don't place small objects in their mouths.

Expand the Activity

· Create a second liquid sensory bottle and eliminate the food coloring. To experiment with light, place the clear sensory bottle in front of an incandescent light or on a light table to observe the difference between the colored bottle and the clear one.

· Discuss the movement of the floating rocks or heavy objects, after the addition of the light.

Build Vocabulary

roll, swirl, bottle, rock, cause and effect, movement, funnel, observe, see, sink, float, up, down, drop, fast, slow

Inquiry Questions and Comments

· We're going to use a funnel to help us pour the oil into the bottle. Do you see it drop down inside the bottle? Let's drop the rock inside.

· What does it sound like when we drop the rock inside the bottle? Do you hear anything? It's quiet; that's correct!

· What do you see inside the bottle?

· What do you see when you shake the bottle?

· How is the rock moving? Does the rock move fast or slow?

Home-School Connection

Invite the parents to replicate the activity at home using small household items.

Suggested Books

· *Bright Baby Colors, ABC, and Numbers First Words* by Roger Priddy

· *Bubbles, Bubbles* by Kathi Appelt

· *First 100 Words (Bright Baby)* by Roger Priddy

· *My Five Senses* by Aliki

· *My Five Senses* by Margaret Miller

· *Richard Scarry's Best First Book Ever!* by Richard Scarry

Look What Absorbs!

Ages

○ **Infants**

● **Toddlers**

● **Twos**

STEM Concepts

● **Science** (Physical science)

● **Technology** (Simple tools)

○ **Engineering**

● **Math** (Number sense and operations)

Learning Outcomes

Children will have opportunities to explore how different materials absorb water and the rate at which the water is absorbed.

Teaching Tips

Absorption is the process by which one substance takes up another substance, or is absorbed. Some materials and surfaces allow for absorption, while others do not. Water will be absorbed at different rates depending on the texture and surface of the object.

Materials

• magnifying glasses

• eyedroppers

• small container of water

• plastic tray

• materials to test absorption, such as paper towels, small white paper plates, white coffee filters, cotton balls, aluminum foil, wax paper, sponges, plastic storage lids, small plastic toys

• clipboard

• towels for cleanup

Getting Ready

Collect items for testing and examining. Demonstrate to the children how to use a magnifying glass and an eyedropper.

How To

Fill a plastic container with water. Select a variety of different materials, such as small white paper plates, white coffee filters, cotton balls, aluminum foil, wax paper, and plastic storage lids, to test to see if they will absorb water or not and place on a plastic tray. Let the children examine and discuss each of the materials prior to testing. Share with the children how the different objects feel. Have the children use a magnifying glass to examine the objects up close. Ask the children which objects they hypothesize will absorb the water. Document the children's predictions and findings on the clipboard.

Invite the children to use the eyedroppers to drip water on the objects. Invite the children to investigate how water changes or doesn't change the surface of the object. Line all the different materials on a table and discuss what children experienced. Count the number of objects that absorb water and those that did not. Document the children's comments and findings on your clipboard.

Hint: Be sure to closely supervise young children to make sure they don't place small objects in their mouths.

Expand the Activity

- Place a few drops of one food coloring in a small container of water. Ask the children to make predictions about what might happen as they add a second color to the water. Discuss that the two colors blend and get absorbed in the water. Discuss with the children what color they made when they added two colors together. For example, red and yellow will make orange.

- Have the children go for a hunt around the room to see what additional materials they would like to test for water absorption. Ask if they think the cement walkway will absorb the water. Ask the children if their skin will absorb water or not. Test out their answers.

Build Vocabulary

small, white, paper plates, coffee filters, cotton balls, aluminum foil, wax paper, plastic lids, absorb, absorption, hypothesize, investigate, test, eyedroppers, magnifying glass, drip, change, surface

Inquiry Questions and Comments

- We're going to look at absorption today. Absorption is when one material takes up another one. Let's look at these different objects. I'll chart on this clipboard what you see.

- Which ones do you think will get absorbed?

- How did the material change?

- How does it feel when it's wet?

- Which ones didn't absorb the water?

- What happened to the water when we dropped the green food coloring in it?

- How did the materials change with the green food coloring?

- Does it feel different than before?

Home-School Connection

During bath time, talk about water absorption. Let children pick items to play with in the tub that will sink, float, and absorb water.

Suggested Books

- *Baby Polar Bear* by Aubrey Lang and Wayne Lynch

- *Bright Baby Colors, ABC, and Numbers First Words* by Roger Priddy

- *Bubbles, Bubbles* by Kathi Appelt

- *First 100 Words (Bright Baby)* by Roger Priddy

- *My Five Senses* by Aliki

- *My Five Senses* by Margaret Miller

- *Richard Scarry's Best First Book Ever!* by Richard Scarry

- *Tacky the Penguin* by Helen Lester

Mirror, Mirror on the Wall

Ages

○ **Infants**

● **Toddlers**

● **Twos**

STEM Concepts

● **Science** (Physical science)

○ **Technology**

○ **Engineering**

○ **Math**

Learning Outcomes

Children will gain an understanding of reflection and of blending and mixing colors. They will explore their senses as they paint with their hands.

Teaching Tips

Mixing two or three separate colors together creates a new color. The proportion of one color to another will affect the outcome of the color. For example, equal parts of blue and yellow will make green.

Materials

• large framed mirror

• drop cloth or plastic tablecloth

• washable tempera paints

• small plastic containers

• paintbrushes

Getting Ready

Secure a large framed mirror either on a wall or against a wall. Place it where there is natural lighting for the children. Place a drop cloth or plastic tablecloth below the mirror. Place washable tempera paints in a small plastic containers.

How To

Children will be mixing colors to get new colors by painting on the mirror. They can use their hands or paintbrushes to paint. At first, the children will see their reflection in the mirror, but eventually, the mirror will be covered with paint.

Hint: For young toddlers, use an acrylic mirror for this activity. The acrylic mirror is lighter and shatter resistant.

Expand the Activity

- When the children have finished painting and the paint is still wet, create a monoprint. Do this by placing a piece of white construction paper against the wet mirror and rubbing the back of the paper. As you gently pull the paper away from the mirror, you will see a copy of the original art.

- When the paint has dried, give the children sponges and water to clean the mirror. The cleanup can be as fun as the painting!

Build Vocabulary

mirror, reflection, paint, cold, sticky, wet, mix, colors, together

Inquiry Questions and Comments

- Today we're going to paint on something different. We're going to use a mirror instead of paper.

- What do you think it will be like to paint on the mirror?

- What two colors would you like to use?

- As you paint, you will see the colors mix together.

- As the colors mix together, they will change colors. The red and yellow will make orange. The red and blue will make purple.

- Let's see what colors you'll make.

- Oh, look! Your two colors are changing. What color did you make?

- What does it feel like to use your hands?

Home-School Connection

Send home paint and two pieces of paper. Let the children paint and create a monoprint.

Suggested Books

- *Baby Touch and Feel: Colors and Shapes* by DK Publishing

- *Baby Touch and Feel: Numbers* by DK Publishing

- *Bright Baby Colors, ABC, and Numbers* by Roger Priddy

- *First 100 Numbers Colors Shapes (Bright Baby)* by Roger Priddy

- *Mouse Paint* by Ellen Stoll Walsh

- *My Crayons Talk* by Patricia Hubbard

- *My Very First Book of Numbers* by Eric Carle

- *White Rabbit's Color Box* by Alan Baker

Move and Groove to the Music

Ages

● Infants

● Toddlers

● Twos

STEM Concepts

● **Science** (Physical science, Life science)

○ **Technology**

○ **Engineering**

● **Math** (Patterns, Spatial relationships)

Learning Outcomes

Children will gain an understanding of spatial awareness and how to move their bodies to music.

Teaching Tips

Music is a medium to learn about beat, rhythm, and ways to express yourself through movement and dance.

Materials

• MP3 or CD player

• MP3s or CDs of music with various tempos, from slow to fast

Getting Ready

No additional preparation is needed.

How To

Talk to the children about how they can dance by twisting and twirling their bodies. Demonstrate these physical motions for the children. You may first want to twirl children under your arm or help them learn to twirl on their own. Turn on the music and let them twist and twirl their bodies to music. Children love to move their bodies to music and will enjoy watching the adults join them in this activity. Alternate the tempo and beat of the music, allowing children to move slower or faster depending on the beat of the music. Ask the children if they think the music will be fast or slow. Be sure to allow enough space between children that they don't bump into each other. Adults can hold and move with babies while participating in this activity. Describe to the babies what you're doing.

Expand the Activity

• After playing fast music, ask the children to put their hands on their hearts to feel it beating fast.

• Ask the children to pick out their favorite musical instrument to march and beat to the music.

• At circle time, ask children to pick a friend to dance with them while the rest of the children watch and clap to the music. Let children take turns dancing in the circle.

Build Vocabulary

twist, twirl, turn, beat, clap, music, movement, fast, slow, bump, neighbor

Inquiry Questions and Comments

- Moving, twisting, and twirling your body is fun to do. Physical movement is healthy for our bodies.

- Watch me as I twist to the music. I'm going to turn on the music fast and we can twist and turn to it. Be careful not to bump into your neighbor. Join me in twisting and turning.

- Does the music sound fast or slow?

- Place your hand on your heart and feel it beating.

Home-School Connection

Invite parents to play music and join their children in the fun of moving and grooving.

Suggested Books

- *Barnyard Dance* by Sandra Boynton

- *Dancing Feet* by Lindsey Craig

- *Giraffes Can't Dance* by Giles Andreae and Guy Parker-Rees

- *Hippos Go Berserk!* by Sandra Boynton

- *My First Body* by DK Publishing

- *Tap Tap Bang Bang* by Emma Garcia

- *Zoom, Zoom, Baby!* by Karen Katz

Muffin, Muffin, Who's Got the Muffin?

Ages

- ● **Infants**
- ● **Toddlers**
- ● **Twos**

STEM Concepts

- ○ **Science**
- ○ **Technology**
- ○ **Engineering**
- ● **Math** (Number Sense, Classification, Spatial relationships)

Learning Outcomes

Children will be introduced to number sense and one-to-one correspondence while working on their fine-motor skills.

Teaching Tips

Children learn one-to-one correspondence and number sense as they align or match one item to another object. As toddlers play with like items, they are sorting and classifying objects by similar or dissimilar attributes.

Materials

- 2 muffin tins
- 12 small objects that are age appropriate and fit inside a muffin cup
- small bowl

Getting Ready

Select twelve objects that are different colors, shapes, and textures, including ones that make noise too. Place them all in a small bowl. Put the muffin tins on a flat surface.

How To

Children are going to be moving objects from one muffin cup to another one. Invite the children to pick up the objects with their hands and place them into the individual muffin cups. Then they can pick up the objects and move them into a new muffin cup.

Hint: It is developmentally appropriate for younger children to place several objects into one muffin cup. Be sure to closely supervise young children to make sure they don't place small objects in their mouths.

Expand the Activity

- Count with the children as they place the objects in each of the muffin cups.

- Place a solid-color sticker on the bottom of each muffin cup and number them from 1 to 12. Invite the children to count the objects as they place them in the muffin cups.

Build Vocabulary

muffin tin, cup, place, object, count

Inquiry Questions and Comments

- This is a muffin tin. It has twelve cups.
- Let's place the objects in the cup.
- Let's count together.
- Where are you going to start?
- What does this object feel like?
- How is this object different than the others?

Home-School Connection

Invite the family to bake muffins or cupcakes and ask the child to place the muffin papers in each cup.

Suggested Books

- *Baby Touch and Feel: Numbers* by DK Publishing
- *Bright Baby Colors, ABC, and Numbers* by Roger Priddy
- *Counting in the Garden* by Kim Parker
- *Counting Kisses: A Kiss and Read Book* by Karen Katz
- *Counting 1 to 20* by Rebecca Bondor
- *First 100 Numbers Colors Shapes (Bright Baby)* by Roger Priddy
- *Mouse Paint* by Ellen Stoll Walsh
- *My Crayons Talk* by Patricia Hubbard
- *My Very First Book of Numbers* by Eric Carle
- *White Rabbit's Color Box* by Alan Baker

My Five Senses

Ages

- ● Infants
- ● Toddlers
- ● Twos

STEM Concepts

- ● **Science** (Physical science, Life science, Earth science)
- ● **Technology** (Simple tools)
- ○ **Engineering**
- ● **Math** (Number sense and operations, Classification, Measurement)

Learning Outcomes

Children will explore their senses as they see, feel, smell, listen, and taste a variety of materials.

Teaching Tips

Children learn through their five senses. Providing sensory-rich activities helps children learn about the characteristics and properties of different objects.

Materials

- variety of sensory objects, including fruits and vegetables, flowers, leaves, wood, and bells
- basket or tray
- magnifying glass
- knife

Getting Ready

Place the sensory items in a basket or on a tray. Cut fruit and cooked vegetables into bite-size pieces and place on a tray.

How To

Introduce the children to the five senses and how we use our ears, eyes, nose, and mouths to learn about the world. Pass the sensory items around one at a time on a tray for the children to touch and feel. Let children look at the objects on the tray with a magnifying glass.

Ask the children if they want to play a sensory game. One at a time, ask the children to either close their eyes or cover their eyes with their hands. Place an object, such as a strawberry or an orange slice, under their nose and see if they can guess what it is. Continue this game with other objects that require using all five senses. Explain how we have different likes and dislikes as to what we taste and smell.

Hint: Children have different sensitivities to how objects smell and feel. Some children may not be ready to explore new items, which is developmentally age appropriate. Just introduce the items and let children explore if they wish.

Expand the Activity

- Take the children on a nature walk. Stop and examine different items and have the children explore them with their senses. Collect the objects and place them in a basket or on a tray in a location where the children can easily examine them.

- Gather a variety of musical instruments and let the children explore the feel and sound of each instrument.

- Have the children smell baking extracts, such as vanilla, almond, or orange, by placing a few drops on a cotton ball. Describe the objects and scents, and help the children make connections with their senses.

Building Vocabulary

five senses, close, cover, ears, eyes, nose, tongue, fingers

Inquiry Questions and Comments

- Let's explore some things through our five senses. Our senses are what we hear, see, smell, taste, and touch.

- What do you hear when I play the bell? Does this bell sound the same or different?

- How does it sound different from the jingle bell?

- With our fingers we feel things. How does the leaf feel?

- Listen to it as I crunch it between my fingers.

- How does the strawberry taste? Is it sweet or sour?

Home-School Connection

Invite parents to introduce the child to a new food this week.

Suggested Books

- *Apples and Pumpkins* by Anne Rockwell

- *The Apple Pie Tree* by Zoe Hall

- *Bright Baby Touch and Feel Baby Animals* by Roger Priddy

- *Don't Touch, It's Hot (Touch and Feel)* by David Algrim and Holli Conger

- *Eating the Alphabet: Fruits and Vegetables from A to Z* by Lois Ehlert

- *Food from Farms* by Nancy Dickmann

- *From the Garden: A Counting Book about Growing Food* by Michael Dahl and Todd Ouren

- *How Are You Peeling?* by Saxton Freymann

- *The Little Mouse, the Red Ripe Strawberry, and the Big Hungry Bear* by Don Wood and Audrey Wood

- *Mouse Shapes* by Ellen Stoll Walsh

- *Mouse Paint* by Ellen Stoll Walsh

- *My Five Senses* by Aliki

- *My Five Senses* by Margaret Miller

- *White Rabbit's Color Box* by Alan Baker

One, Two, That's My Shoe

Ages

○ Infants
● Toddlers
● Twos

STEM Concepts

○ Science
○ Technology
○ Engineering
● Math (Number sense and operations, Patterns and classification)

Learning Outcomes

Children will gain an understanding of number sense and operations as they count, sort, and match shoes.

Teaching Tips

The concepts of number sense and operations are introduced as children count, sort, and classify items. They learn about the concepts of same and different as they play and explore with like items.

Materials

• children's shoes

• dress-up shoes, such as boots, high heels, or slippers

• 2 medium-size baskets.

Getting Ready

No additional preparation is needed.

How To

Have the children take off their shoes. Show the children each shoe and how they are similar or different. Identify them by color, type, and if they have laces or Velcro, among other attributes. Invite the children to place one shoe in each basket. The teacher will need to model this step for younger children. You may want to add some of the dress-up shoes in the basket too. One by one, let children pick out their own shoes from each basket, and then have them match the other children's shoes. Return all the shoes to their original basket before the next child takes his turn.

Expand the Activity

Invite the children to sort the shoes and create AB patterns.

Build Vocabulary

shoes, match, same, different, leather, boots, tennis shoes, laces, Velcro, tie, sole, toe, heel, feet

Inquiry Questions and Comments

- There are different kinds of shoes. We wear a shoe on each of our feet. Let's look at our shoes.
- Now look at your neighbor's shoes. Are they the same or different from yours?
- What do we see when we look at the shoes?
- How are the shoes the same?
- How are they different?

Home-School Connection

Invite parents to have children help set the dinner table and sort silverware.

Suggested Books

- *1, 2, Buckle My Shoe* by Anna Grossnickle Hines
- *Baby Touch and Feel: Numbers* by DK Publishing
- *Bright Baby Colors, ABC, and Numbers* by Roger Priddy
- *Counting in the Garden* by Kim Parker
- *Counting Kisses: A Kiss and Read Book* by Karen Katz
- *Counting 1 to 20* by Rebecca Bondor
- *Gray Rabbit's 1, 2, 3* by Alan Baker

Ooh La La Oobleck

Ages

○ Infants

● Toddlers

● Twos

STEM Concepts

● **Science** (Physical science)

● **Technology** (Simple tools)

○ **Engineering**

○ **Math**

Learning Outcomes

Children will explore physical science as they combine solids and liquids and experience the changes in these two materials.

Teaching Tips

The foundation of physical science is to investigate the characteristics and physical properties of nonliving objects and of solid and liquid materials. Oobleck is a non-Newtonian fluid. It has the properties of both liquids and solids.

Materials

- plastic tablecloth
- cornstarch
- water
- large mixing bowl or sensory table
- measuring cup
- mixing spoon
- pitcher
- painting aprons or old shirts
- bucket of water and towels for cleanup

Getting Ready

Oobleck is great as both an indoor or outdoor activity, but it can be a bit messy. Be sure to cover the table and workspace with a plastic tablecloth. Have a bucket of water and towels handy for cleanup. Place the Oobleck on a table or flat surface so it's easy for children to reach their hands into the bowl.

How To

To make the Oobleck, measure one part water to two parts cornstarch. First pour the water into the bowl, then spoon in the cornstarch, a little bit at a time. The mixing bowl or sensory table should be large enough to allow several children to play at the same time. Let the children begin to mix the materials together with the spoon or their hands until it reaches a gooey consistency. Encourage children to grab a handful of Oobleck and squeeze it. It will ooze out of their fingers. They can roll it into a ball and it will become solid. When they let go, it will melt back in their hands. Place a pitcher in the Oobleck mixture so the children can explore pouring it. Oobleck can be stored in an airtight container.

Hint: Use soap and water for easy cleanup.

Expand the Activity

- After the children have played with the Oobleck, ask them what color or colors they would like to add to the fun. Add a few drops of food coloring into the Oobleck and watch the colors change.

- Because Oobleck can be rinsed off with soap and water, add some plastic animals into the mix.

Build Vocabulary

liquid, solid, mix, mixing spoon, gooey, squeeze, hands, fingers, ooze

Inquiry Questions and Comments

- We're going to mix cornstarch and water together. The cornstarch is a solid and the water is a liquid. Let's pour in the water first. Would you like to help pour in the water?

- Next we're going to slowly pour in the cornstarch, one spoonful at a time. Who'd like to put the cornstarch in?

- How does the Oobleck feel?

- How does it change?

- Is it liquid or solid?

- That's right; it can be both!

Home-School Connection

Share the recipe with parents, and invite them to try this activity at home. Remind them that it can be a bit messy!

Suggested Books

- *Bartholomew and the Oobleck* by Dr. Seuss

- *Baby Touch and Feel: Splish! Splash!* by DK Publishing

- *Bright Baby Touch and Feel Baby Animals* by Roger Priddy

- *My Five Senses* by Aliki

- *My Five Senses* by Margaret Miller

- *Richard Scarry's Best First Book Ever!* by Richard Scarry

Orange Float

Ages

○ **Infants**

○ **Toddlers**

● **Twos**

STEM Concepts

● **Science** (Physical science, Life science)

● **Technology** (Simple tool)

○ **Engineering**

● **Math** (Number sense)

Learning Outcomes

Children will gain experience with the concepts of sink and float.

Teaching Tips

Objects either sink or float, depending on the object's density and mass. The air trapped between the flesh of the orange and the orange peel causes the unpeeled orange to be buoyant and float. Buoyancy is the force that makes an object rise upward when placed in water compared to an object that sinks in water.

Materials

• 2 oranges

• water

• medium-size clear plastic container

• magnifying glass

Getting Ready

Fill a clear plastic container with enough water to allow the oranges to float.

How To

Ask children what they know about oranges. Discuss the color, shape, and taste of them, and describe how oranges grow on trees. Pass around the oranges so children can experience the outside of the orange. Peel one of the oranges, keeping the skin for later investigation. Ask the children to feel and smell the unpeeled orange. Ask the children if they think the orange with its skin on or with its skin off will sink or float. Put both of the oranges in the water. Give the children magnifying glasses to examine the inside of the orange and its peel more closely. Document the children's predictions and the results.

Hint: The outside of the orange is called the *rind* or the *skin*. For this activity, the word *skin* will be used. Air gets trapped between the flesh and skin, allowing the orange to float.

Expand the Activity

• After examining the orange peel, break the orange into sections and let the children examine the sections. Share with the children the math concept part to whole.

• Repeat the activity with a large grapefruit.

• Let the children sample orange juice during snacktime.

Build Vocabulary

orange, float, sink, skin, peel, sections, smell, taste, feel

Inquiry Questions and Comments

- Here's an orange. Oranges have a skin on the outside. Let's see what we can observe about its skin.

- How does the skin feel?

- What do you know about oranges?

- What does the orange look like?

- How does the orange feel?

- How does the orange smell?

- Which orange do you think will sink or float? The one with the skin on or the one with the skin off?

- Let's put the oranges in the water. Why do you think this orange floated? Why do you think this orange sank?

Home-School Connection

Invite parents to investigate oranges and other fruit at home with their children. They can discuss what the child observes about the outside of the fruit. Then they can peel or cut open the fruit to see what is underneath the peel or skin. They can discuss their new observations and then eat the fruit to see how it tastes. If they want to take it a step further, they can see if the fruit floats in water with its peel on versus when it is off.

Suggested Books

- *Boats* by Anne Rockwell

- *Boats Board Book* by Byron Barton

- *How Are You Peeling?* by Saxton Freymann

- *Who Sank the Boat?* by Pamela Allen

Pinwheel Straw Blowing

Ages

○ **Infants**

● **Toddlers**

● **Twos**

STEM Concepts

● **Science** (Physical science, Life science)

● **Technology** (Simple tools)

○ **Engineering**

○ **Math**

Learning Outcomes

Children will experience their own breath and how it feels to exhale and move objects using their breath.

Teaching Tips

Children will begin to understand that their breath can cause objects to move through exhalation.

Materials

• pinwheels

• straws

• pom-poms

• feathers

• tray

Getting Ready

No additional preparation is needed.

How To

Let children experience blowing by asking them to place their hand in front of their mouth to feel their exhalation. Let the children watch the flaps of a pinwheel spin as you model how to blow into it. Invite the children to take turns blowing the pinwheel. Share with the children how to blow softly and then with more force. Explain that the flaps will move faster when more force is applied. Model blowing pom-poms using a straw. Place pom-poms and feathers on a tray and let the children use straws to blow the items on the tray. Share with the children that the force of the air from their lungs is moving the objects.

Hint: Be sure to closely supervise young children to make sure they don't place small objects in their mouths.

Expand the Activity

• Invite children to go on a hunt through the classroom to collect items they predict will move when they blow on them.

• Let children practice blowing by playing with bubbles.

Build Vocabulary

blow, hand, straw, breath, breathe, exhale, air, out, lungs, move, spin, pinwheel, feather, pom-pom

Inquiry Questions and Comments

- Put your lips together as you breathe out. Can you feel your breath on your hand? Can you breathe hard? Can you breathe very softly?

- Here's a pinwheel. When we blow on the flaps, it will spin. Let's try it.

- What do you see?

- Let's try blowing through the straw. Can you feel your breath?

- What happens when you blow the straw toward the pom-pom?

- What happens to the feathers when you blow on them?

Home-School Connection

Invite parents to purchase a pinwheel or make one at home with the children. They can have the children practice blowing things around the house with a straw.

Suggested Books

- *Bubbles, Bubbles* by Kathi Appelt

- *Bubbles, Bubbles* by Sesame Street

- *My Five Senses* by Aliki

- *My Five Senses* by Margaret Miller

- *Whistle for Willie* by Ezra Jack Keats

- *The Wind Blew* by Pat Hutchins

- *A Windy Day in Spring* by Charles Ghigna and Laura Watson

Rainbow Jar

Ages

○ **Infants**

○ **Toddlers**

● **Twos**

STEM Concepts

● **Science** (Physical science)

● **Technology** (Simple tools)

● **Engineering** (Engineering)

● **Math** (Number sense and operations, Measurement)

Learning Outcomes

Children will learn about different liquids and how each liquid has a different density. Liquids also feel and smell different.

Teaching Tips

If you pour liquids together, some will mix together, while others won't. If the liquids don't mix together, they will separate because of the density level of the liquid. The liquid with lowest density will be on top, while the liquid with the highest density will stay on the bottom.

Materials

• 6 large, clean, clear glass containers, such as Mason jars

• honey

• blue or green dishwashing soap

• water

• vegetable or olive oil

• rubbing alcohol

• food coloring

• measuring cup

• magnifying glass

Getting Ready

Pour each of the five liquids into a separate container and line them up in this order: honey, dishwashing soap, water, vegetable or olive oil, and rubbing alcohol.

How To

Add food coloring to each of the liquids: purple to honey; blue to the dishwashing soap; green to the water; yellow to the vegetable or olive oil; and red to the rubbing alcohol. When the liquids are added in that order, they will look like a rainbow. Discuss each of the liquids, allowing children to smell and feel all except the rubbing alcohol before adding it to the container. Talk about and document the differences they are experiencing. Measure ⅓–¼ cup of each liquid. First pour the purple honey and then the blue dishwashing soap in the jar. Next, slowly pour the green water down the sides of the jar. Then pour in the yellow vegetable or olive oil and the rubbing alcohol down the sides of the container. Let the children examine the "rainbow" layers with the magnifying glass.

Hint: Make sure the children do not shake the container. The liquids will get mixed together if shaken.

Expand the Activity

Drop a heavy object such as a marble in the liquid and watch it fall through the liquids.

Build Vocabulary

magnifying glass, layer, liquid, oil, honey, dishwashing soap, water, eyedropper, smell, feel, density

Inquiry Questions and Comments

- We're going to pour each of these liquids into this container.

- Each liquid is different. Let's watch and see what happens.

- Let's smell this liquid.

- How does this liquid feel?

- What do you see when we add the next liquid? It is making a new layer of liquid.

- How does this liquid feel compared to that liquid? This liquid is heavier or denser than that one.

- Let's count the colors.

Home-School Connection

Share the list of liquids used in the activity. Invite the parents to show the children how you use these liquids such as dishwashing soap and vegetable and olive oil for everyday cooking and cleaning.

Suggested Books

- *Baby Touch and Feel: Colors and Shapes* by DK Publishing

- *Bright Baby Colors, ABC, and Numbers* by Roger Priddy

- *First 100 Numbers Colors Shapes (Bright Baby)* by Roger Priddy

- *Mouse Paint* by Ellen Stoll Walsh

- *My Crayons Talk* by Patricia Hubbard

- *My Very First Book of Numbers* by Eric Carle

- *National Geographic Little Kids First Big Book of Why* by Catherine Hughes

- *Planting a Rainbow* by Lois Ehlert

- *The Rainbow Fish* by Marcus Pfister and J. Alison James

- *White Rabbit's Color Book* by Alan Baker

Rattle and Shake Sensory Bottle

Ages

- ● **Infants**
- ● **Toddlers**
- ○ **Twos**

STEM Concepts

- ● **Science** (Physical science, Life science, Earth science)
- ● **Technology** (Simple tools)
- ● **Engineering** (Engineer)
- ● **Math** (Classification, Measurement)

Learning Outcomes

Children will examine objects found in the indoor and outdoor environment and experience the sounds the materials make as they rattle and shake the bottles.

Teaching Tips

Life science materials have different properties that can be classified. We can observe and classify different properties of rice, peas, beans, and feathers. By shaking the bottles, children can hear and see the objects moving.

Materials

- 8–10 small plastic containers with lids
- variety of different items, such as uncooked rice, beans, peas, sand, feathers, rocks, dice, beads, small jingle bells, glitter, strips of metallic paper

- several clean, empty 8–12-ounce plastic water bottles
- funnel
- scissors
- colored duct tape

Getting Ready

Select a variety of items that you wish to place in the sensory bottle. Place each individual item in a separate sealed container.

How To

Place the plastic bottle on a flat surface and insert the funnel. Depending on the age of the children, have them take turns holding the bottle while you pour in each item, or you hold the bottle while they pour. Older children can help each other while you supervise. Encourage the children to watch as the items fall through the funnel into the bottle. Cut the colored duct tape and seal the top securely. Let the children examine and shake the sensory bottle. Each separate sensory bottle will sound different based on the items placed in it.

Hint: If you are working with younger children, having the items in individual sealed containers will make this activity easier, and children will not be able to put loose items in their mouths. Small items that make sounds, like small jingle bells, are nice to add, as well as glitter and strips of metallic paper that can reflect light.

Expand the Activity

- Create sensory bottles that have like items in them, such as all buttons or all seashells.

- Create colored sensory bottles such as all red or yellow items. Place a label on the bottle with the name of the color to help children connect the color they see with the written word.

Build Vocabulary

bottle, rice, beans, peas, sand, feathers, rocks, dice, beads, cause and effect, movement, see, hear, observe, steady, drop, down

Inquiry Questions and Comments

- What item is this? That's right; it's a . . .

- We're going to use a funnel to help us pour the rice into the bottle. Do you see it drop down inside the bottle?

- What does it sound like when we drop the rice inside the bottle?

- What do you see inside the bottle?

- What do you hear when you shake the bottle?

Home-School Connection

Invite the parents to replicate the activity at home using small household items.

Suggested Books

- *Bright Baby Colors, ABC, and Numbers First Words* by Roger Priddy

- *Bubbles, Bubbles* by Kathi Appelt

- *First 100 Words (Bright Baby)* by Roger Priddy

- *My Five Senses* by Aliki

- *My Five Senses* by Margaret Miller

- *Richard Scarry's Best First Book Ever!* by Richard Scarry

Ribbon Shakers

Ages

○ **Infants**

● **Toddlers**

● **Twos**

STEM Concepts

● **Science** (Physical science, Life science)

● **Technology** (Simple tools)

○ **Engineering**

● **Math** (Number sense, Measurement)

Learning Outcomes

Children will gain sensory experiences from this activity as they make and shake the bottle, listen to the noise it makes, and see the colors of the ribbons.

Teaching Tips

Children will develop their senses of sight, touch, and hearing by exploring the sensory bottles.

Materials

• ¼-inch-wide satin ribbon in a variety of colors

• scissors

• several clean, empty plastic water bottles (those with colored tops are fun to use)

• screwdriver

• ¼ cup uncooked rice

• small bowl

• colored pom-poms

• funnel

- masking tape or duct tape

- decorative duct tape

- tray, optional

Getting Ready

Cut the ribbon into 12-inch-long pieces. Poke a hole in the top of the bottle top using a screwdriver. Put the rice in a small bowl.

How To

Invite children to investigate the pom-poms and the ribbons. Ask them to share how they look and feel. Place the pom-poms and rice in the bottle using the funnel. Invite children to watch and listen as you do this. Thread three ribbons through the hole in the bottle top and knot them together so they do not slide through the top. Before sealing the top, take a 1–2-inch strip of masking tape or duct tape and tape the ribbon knots down on the inside of the bottle top. Screw on the top. Secure the top to the bottle with decorative duct tape. Let the children shake and move the bottle to music.

Hint: The pom-poms and rice may spill when children are in the process of filling the bottle. You may want to have them pour over a large container or tray for easier cleanup. Be sure to closely supervise young children to make sure they don't place small objects in their mouths.

Expand the Activity

- Let the children use an ice cream scoop to collect rice and drop it into the funnel. Invite them to watch and listen as the rice drops into the bottle.

- Invite the children to use their fingers or tweezers to drop the pom-poms into the bottle.

Build Vocabulary

soft, satin, pom-poms, ribbon, color, rice, knot, hole, shake, noise, top, funnel, tweezers, ice cream scoop

Inquiry Questions and Comments

- What colors of ribbon do you see?

- What colors of pom-poms do you see?

- What does the ribbon feel like?

- As you shake the bottle, can you feel the vibration of the rice and pom-poms inside?

- Let's count the pom-poms as we put them in the bottle.

- What does it sound like when you shake the bottle?

- What happens to the ribbons when you move the bottle back and forth?

Home-School Connection

Invite parents to make a sensory bottle at home with items found around the house. Ribbons are optional. Remind them to be sure to secure the top with duct tape.

Suggested Books

- *Bright Baby Colors, ABC, and Numbers First Words* by Roger Priddy

- *First 100 Words (Bright Baby)* by Roger Priddy

- *My Five Senses* by Aliki

- *My Five Senses* by Margaret Miller

- *Richard Scarry's Best First Book Ever!* by Richard Scarry

Ring the Bells

Ages

- Infants
- Toddlers
- Twos

STEM Concepts

- **Science** (Physical science, Earth science)
- **Technology** (Simple tool)
- **Engineering** (Engineering)
- **Math** (Classification)

Learning Outcomes

Children will gain an understanding of different types of bells and the sound each one makes. They will gain an understanding of how wind and motion impacts the sound of the clapper and the sound of the bells.

Teaching Tips

The bells and wind chimes have a clapper that makes sounds when it hits the outside of the bell or chime.

Materials

variety of bells (such as jingle bells, school bells, and cow bells), wind chimes, and whistles

Getting Ready

Hang a wind chime outside and have the children listen to the sound it makes in the wind.

How To

Let the children hold, feel, and hear each bell and whistle. Talk about the different sounds they make. Explain that bells and wind chimes have a clapper, and when it strikes the sides, a sound is made. Ring the bells softly first and then loudly. Explain how a whistle works and how it sounds different than bells.

Hint: Some children are sensitive to noise. You may want to do this activity outside. Be sure to closely supervise young children to make sure they don't place small objects in their mouths.

Expand the Activity

- Make handbells by cutting a paper towel tube in half. Cover it with contact paper. The contact paper will make it stronger and more durable. Punch two holes in each end of the tube about an inch from the edge. Tie two jingle bells to a piece of yarn and then thread the yarn through the holes. Let the children decorate the outside of the bells with markers or stickers. Shake to play.

- Use a bell as a cue for transitions.

Build Vocabulary

bells, wind chimes, clapper, ring, wind, hang, noise, loud, soft, sound

Inquiry Questions and Comments

- We're going to look at a lot of different bells today. They all make different sounds when we ring them. Let's listen to the sound of this bell.

- Does the jingle bell sound the same as or different than the handbell?

- What happens when we ring the two bells at the same time?

- Which bell do you like best? Why?

- Would you like to ring the bell?

Home-School Connection

Invite parents to talk to their children about the bells and whistles in their home. Ask the children to bring bells and whistles from home to share at school the next day.

Suggested Books

- *What Is the Weather Today?* by Rebecca Bondor

- *What Makes the Seasons?* by Megan Montague Cash

- *Whistle for Willie* by Ezra Jack Keats

- *The Wind Blew* by Pat Hutchins

- *A Windy Day in Spring* by Charles Ghigna and Laura Watson

Roll the Die

Ages

- ● **Infants**
- ● **Toddlers**
- ● **Twos**

STEM Concepts

- ● **Science** (Physical science)
- ○ **Technology**
- ○ **Engineering**
- ● **Math** (Number sense, Shapes)

Learning Outcomes

Children will practice rolling the die to gain an understanding of motion and speed. Children will experience rolling a giant die while practicing shape recognition.

Teaching Tips

Motion is the act or process of moving. In this activity, sit with the children and roll the die back and forth. With older children, talk about each shape one at a time. Use your finger to outline the edges of each shape.

Materials

- square box, at least 6 × 6 × 6 inches, with a lid
- white paper
- clear packing tape
- colored construction paper
- 2 or 3 wiffle balls

Getting Ready

Cover the box and lid separately with white paper and secure with packing tape. Cut out six different 4-inch shapes, each of a different color construction paper, and tape one to each side to make the die.

How To

With the children's help, place two or three wiffle balls inside the box, close the lid, and secure with packing tape. Sit on the ground with the infant or toddler, and roll the die back and forth. Talk to the infants and toddlers about the sound the die makes when it is rolled or shaken. Talk about what shape you see.

Hint: The larger the box, the easier it will be for little hands to roll!

Expand the Activity

- Older children can roll the die with a friend or with others during group time. Have them practice identifying the shapes.

- For older twos and threes, make a similar box. This one will have numbers on it instead of shapes. Cut out colored numbers 1 through 6 and tape them on each side of the die.

Build Vocabulary

sides, square, circle, rectangle, triangle, oval, star, die, roll

Inquiry Questions and Comments

- Let's look at the shapes. This one is a square. It's red. This one is a triangle. What color is it? Blue, that's right!

- Let's roll the die, and listen to how it sounds.

- What do you hear when I roll it to you?

- What colors do you see?

Home-School Connection

Invite parents to go on a color and shape hunt in the house, helping children identify and practice their colors and shapes.

Suggested Books

- *Baby's Shapes* by Karen Katz

- *Baby Touch and Feel: Colors and Shapes* by DK Publishing

- *Brown Rabbit's Shape Book* by Alan Baker

- *First 100 Numbers Colors Shapes (Bright Baby)* by Roger Priddy

- *Gray Rabbit's 1, 2, 3* by Alan Baker

- *Shapes, Shapes, Shapes* by Tana Hoban

Rolling and Racing

Ages

○ **Infants**

○ **Toddlers**

● **Twos**

STEM Concepts

● **Science** (Physical science)

● **Technology** (Simple machines, Simple tools)

● **Engineering** (Engineering)

● **Math** (Measurement, Mathematical reasoning)

Learning Outcomes

Children will experience motion, force, gravity, speed, and distance as they build and play with ramps and inclined planes.

Teaching Tips

Changing the elevation of an incline ramp will affect the speed and distance objects will roll.

Materials

• 1-inch-diameter foam pipe insulation, 4–5-inch-diameter drain coupler, or cardboard or plastic tubes, 4 inches or larger in diameter

• scissors or box cutter

• small balls or toy cars

• masking tape

• beanbags or small pillows

• paper towel cardboard tube, optional

Getting Ready

Create the ramps by using cardboard or plastic tubes, foam pipe insulation, or drain couplers (available at hardware stores). If using foam pipe insulation, cut each 6-foot piece in half lengthwise using a scissors or box cutter. This will create 6 feet of open ramps for the children to roll items down.

How To

Start by placing the end of one of the ramp pieces on a low table or on the back of a chair. Model how to drop the small ball or toy from the top of the piece and let the children watch it roll down the ramp. Let the children play and experiment with rolling the balls down the ramp.

Next, tape two pieces of foam pipe insulation together to make a 12-foot ramp. Place the top of the ramp on a higher elevation, such as on a table or the back of a chair to increase the inclined plane. Place small beanbags or a small pillow under the ramp to engineer hills and small inclined planes for the ball to go over. As the children explore and roll the balls down the ramp, measure how far the balls travel past the end of the ramp or place a paper towel cardboard tube at the end of the ramp for the balls to travel through.

Hint: Be sure to closely supervise young children to make sure they don't place small objects in their mouths.

Expand the Activity

• Add an additional 6-foot piece of insulation and engineer a loop for the ball to roll through.

You can add stability to the loop by placing additional beanbags or pillows on either side of it.

- Share with the children that inclined planes are found in our everyday world. Point out inclined planes, such as slides, stairs, ramps, ladders, or dump trucks, as you see them on walks or in your classroom.

Build Vocabulary

place, ball, ramp, foam, under, speed, fast, slow, roll, engineer, measure, distance, hill

Inquiry Questions and Comments

- We're going to engineer a ramp today. Let's see how fast and how far the ball rolls down the ramp.

- Let's measure to see how far it rolled.

- What do you think will happen if we raise the top of the ramp? Let's see what happens.

- What do you think will happen if we lower the top of the ramp? Does the ball roll faster or slower?

- What do you think will happen when we tape two pieces together?

- Where should we build a hill?

- What happens when we place the beanbag under the ramp?

- What does the ball do now?

Home-School Connection

Invite parents to roll and bounce balls with children. Ask them to identify incline planes, such as slides, stairs, ramps, ladders, or dump trucks, in their yards or neighborhoods.

Suggested Books

- *Big Board First 100 Machines* by Roger Priddy
- *Big Book of Things That Go* by DK Publishing
- *Big and Little: Things That Go* by Rebecca Bondor
- *Bridges: Amazing Structures to Design, Build, and Test* by Carol A. Johmann
- *First 100 Trucks (Bright Baby)* by Roger Priddy
- *Let's Count Trucks: A Fun Kids' Counting Book for Toddler Boys and Children Age 2 to 5* by Alina Niemi
- *Look at That Building* by Scot Ritchie
- *The World's Most Amazing Bridges* by Michael Hurley

Sand, Sieves, and Shovels

Ages

○ **Infants**

● **Toddlers**

● **Twos**

STEM Concepts

● **Science** (Physical science, Life science, Earth science)

● **Technology** (Simple tools)

○ **Engineering**

● **Math** (Number sense and operations, Measurement, Spatial relationships)

Learning Outcomes

Children will learn the properties of sand and mathematical concepts, and will have the sensory experience of playing in the sand.

Teaching Tips

Children learn the different properties of physical, life, and earth sciences as they dig and play in the sand.

Materials

• outdoor sand area or a large plastic container of sand

• assortment of items for filling and dumping, such as plastic storage containers, measuring cups, buckets, sieves, spoons, sand and water wheels, and shovels

• small toys to add to the sand play, such as plastic farm animals, cars, trucks, ABC blocks, and large pegs

Getting Ready

No additional preparation is needed.

How To

Toddlers, twos, and three-year-olds love to play with sand, filling containers with items and then dumping them out. Place all of the assorted items in the outdoor sand play area. If you don't have an outdoor sand area, you can use a large plastic container for this activity. Demonstrate to younger children how you fill objects with sand and then how to dump them out. Provide a variety of items for children to explore filling and pouring out the sand. Sieves and sand and water wheel toys provide additional exploration on gravity and motion.

Hint: Be sure to closely supervise young children to make sure they don't place small objects in their mouths.

Expand the Activity

- The teacher could pour a cup of water into the sand area and talk about how the properties of sand change when it gets wet.

- Ask the children to sort and count the items with you.

Build Vocabulary

fill, dump, pour, top, empty, feel, count, measuring cups, plastic containers

Inquiry Questions and Comments

- Let's dig in the sand today. Help me dump out all the toys. Watch as I fill the buckets and sieves with sand. How much sand could we put in our bucket? Is it full yet?

- Let's count how many shovels we have.

- You can use a shovel or large spoon to fill the containers. There are toys here you can use too!

- Listen to the sound it makes when I dump the sand out. What does it sound like?

- Here's a bucket for you. What do you want to put in your bucket?

- What does it feel like to have the sand drop through your fingers?

Home-School Connection

Invite parents to take their child to a park where there is sand and bring along large wooden spoons, plastic storage containers and other materials for sand play.

Suggested Books

- *Baby Touch and Feel: Animals* by DK Publishing

- *Bright Baby Colors, ABC, and Numbers First Words* by Roger Priddy

- *Dig Dig Digging* by Margaret Mayo

- *Let's Count Trucks: A Fun Kids' Counting Book for Toddler Boys and Children Age 2 to 5* by Alina Niemi

- *My Five Senses* by Aliki

- *My Five Senses* by Margaret Miller

- *Sally in the Sand* by Stephen Huneck

- *Tip Tip Dig Dig* by Emma Garcia

Shape Beanbag Toss

Ages

○ **Infants**

○ **Toddlers**

● **Twos**

STEM Concepts

● **Science** (Physical science, Life science)

○ **Technology**

○ **Engineering**

● **Math** (Number sense, Shapes, Spatial relationships)

Learning Outcomes

Children will gain an understanding of the physical science properties of motion, gravity, and force. They will also gain experience with spatial relationships and number sense.

Teaching Tips

As children learn to aim and toss the beanbags, they experience the principle that an increase in force causes an increase in motion.

Materials

• colored construction paper

• masking or painter's tape

• scissors

• colored beanbags

Getting Ready

Cut construction paper into different shapes approximately 6 inches square. For example, a red star, a yellow rectangle, and a blue square.

How To

Identify the shapes with the children before they begin the game. Talk to them about the properties of each shape; for example, a square has four even sides and four corners. Spread out the shapes on the play area and tape them to the floor. Explain to the children that they are going to aim and throw the beanbag at a shape, such as at the red star. Invite the children to line up a few feet from the shapes. Model how to toss the beanbags toward the shapes. Identify the color of each beanbag for the child and count the beanbags as they are tossed. You can purchase beanbags with numbers written on them, which can be identified too.

Hint: You may want to laminate the shapes to make them more durable. This allows you to repeat the game many times. Before you begin the game, have the children practice tossing the beanbags without using the shapes. This allows them to gain a sense of the weight of the beanbag and what it feels like to throw it. Young children will throw underhand and may not hit the star at first, but with practice they will learn how to toss the beanbags with more accuracy.

Expand the Activity

• Cut a second set of similar shapes and have the children match the shapes.

- Use sidewalk chalk to draw shapes on the cement in the outdoor space and let children repeat the activity.

Build Vocabulary

circle, star, toss, aim, beanbag, mark, sheet, hit, miss

Inquiry Questions and Comments

- What shapes do you see? That's right, there's a red star and a blue square. We're going to toss the beanbags toward the star.

- We don't have to throw too hard to make it land in the circle.

- Let's see how far you can throw it.

- What happens if you throw it really hard?

- What happens when you throw it gently?

- What shape did it land on?

Home-School Connection

Invite parents to play a game of toss the ball with their children at home. Children need to practice the motion of throwing in order to gain hand-eye coordination.

Suggested Books

- *Baby Touch and Feel: Colors and Shapes* by DK Publishing

- *Baby Touch and Feel: Numbers* by DK Publishing

- *Big Book of Things That Go* by DK Publishing

- *Big and Little: Things That Go* by Rebecca Bondor

- *Bright Baby Colors, ABC, and Numbers* by Roger Priddy

- *First 100 Numbers Colors Shapes (Bright Baby)* by Roger Priddy

- *My Very First Book of Numbers* by Eric Carle

Sidewalk Chalk

Ages

○ **Infants**

○ **Toddlers**

● **Twos**

STEM Concepts

● **Science** (Physical science)

● **Technology** (Simple tools)

○ **Engineering**

● **Math** (Number sense and operations, Measurement)

Learning Outcomes

Children will learn about the properties of water as they help make homemade sidewalk chalk.

Teaching Tips

Water is a natural substance that exists in three states: liquid, solid, and gas. Adding materials such as food coloring and cornstarch to water and then freezing it will create a solid that can be used as chalk.

Materials

• cornstarch

• water

• food coloring

• Popsicle or ice cube molds

• measuring cups

• glass measuring cup

• spoon

• dishwashing soap, optional

Getting Ready

No additional preparation is needed.

How To

With the children, measure equal parts water and cornstarch. Two cups of cornstarch and 2 cups of water will be enough to fill several ice cube molds. Mix cornstarch and water together in a glass measuring cup, allowing children to see the changes in the mixture and pour into ice cube or Popsicle molds. Let children drop food coloring into the molds and stir with a spoon. Freeze liquid mixture overnight. Unmold the chalk and let the children play with it outdoors.

Hint: You can add a few drops of liquid dish-washing soap to the cornstarch mixture for easy cleanup.

Expand the Activity

• Add ¼ teaspoon baking soda to each sidewalk chalk mold before placing it in the freezer. When the children are playing with the chalk, spray the chalk marks with vinegar and watch it fizz and bubble.

• Make a larger amount of colored sidewalk mixture and freeze in larger individual freezer containers. After the mixture is frozen, unmold and stack the containers one on top of the other. Let the children watch as the frozen chalk mixture melts and colors blend together.

• Place nontoxic glitter in the molds before freezing.

Build Vocabulary

sidewalk chalk, colors, food coloring, water, cornstarch, freeze, mix, stir, pour, mold, unmold, cold, drop, liquid, frozen

Inquiry Questions and Comments

• We're going to make homemade sidewalk chalk today and then place it in the freezer overnight. Tomorrow we can play with it outside.

• Let's measure the water using the measuring cup. Can you help me by holding the cup?

• Let's take turns stirring the mixture. Who would like to go first?

• Let's take turns pouring the chalk mixture into the molds. Who would like to go first?

• What color do you want to add to the mold?

• How does the chalk feel in your hand? Is it cold?

• Try and draw on the sidewalk with your chalk. What colors do you see?

• What's happening to the chalk? Is it melting?

Home-School Connection

Invite parents to make sidewalk chalk at home.

Suggested Books

• *Baby Touch and Feel: Colors and Shapes* by DK Publishing

• *Bright Baby Colors, ABC, and Numbers First Words* by Roger Priddy

• *First 100 Numbers Colors Shapes (Bright Baby)* by Roger Priddy

• *My Five Senses* by Aliki

• *My Five Senses* by Margaret Miller

• *White Rabbit's Color Book* by Alan Baker

Squeeze, Sparkle, and Shine

Ages

○ **Infants**

● **Toddlers**

● **Twos**

STEM Concepts

● **Science** (Physical science)

● **Technology** (Simple tools)

● **Engineering** (Engineering)

● **Math** (Number sense and operation)

Learning Outcomes

Children will deepen their understanding of light, density, and transparency as they observe and squeeze objects inside a plastic bag. They will explore how the objects look when placed near light.

Teaching Tips

Children will explore the properties and characteristics of different materials as they squeeze and manipulate the objects inside each bag. Children will explore and investigate varying degrees of density and transparency using a natural light or a light table.

Materials

- small items to place in the bag, such as buttons, wiggly eyes, small plastic toys, or seashells

- 1 gallon resealable freezer bag

- clear or colored hair gel

- glitter

- electrical tape

- magnifying glass

- window or light table

Getting Ready

Gather items to place inside the resealable bag. Select five to ten items for each bag, such as small pieces of lace, buttons, wiggly eyes, foam alphabet or number pieces, plastic farm animals, or seashells. Avoid anything with sharp edges that might slice the plastic bag. Place items in the resealable freezer bag and then add the hair gel and glitter. The hair gel and glitter will add to the transparency and sparkle of the bag. The hair gel can be purchased at discount stores and comes clear or in a variety of colors. Squeeze as much of the air out of the bag as possible and seal it. Secure all edges and corners of the bag with electrical tape, which can be found in a variety of colors and patterns.

How To

Share the bags with the children and let the children examine them. Invite the children to squeeze the bags and observe how the items move around. Invite the children to place the bag against a window or on a light table and talk about what they see. They can use a magnifying glass to get a closer look at the items in the bag.

Hint: Be sure and use high-quality freezer bags, which are heavier and more durable, for this activity. Make several different bags so children can compare and contrast the items in the bags. Using colored hair gel or adding a few drops of food coloring to clear gel can add to the uniqueness of each squeeze bag. Be sure to closely supervise young children to make sure they don't place small objects in their mouths.

Expand the Activity

- Place a variety of items for the bags in small bowls. Invite the children to make their own bags by picking the items they want for the bags. The teacher should place the hair gel and glitter in the bag and seal it. Invite the children to pick the kind of electrical tape they want to use on their bag. Let the children observe the bags by squeezing them and placing them against a window or on a light table to see the light shine through them.

- Send the bag home for a home-school activity.

- Invite parents to have the children draw a picture of the bag and write down what the children say about exploring the activity.

Build Vocabulary

bag, clear, seal, plastic, glitter, squeeze, sparkle, move, see, light, window, light table

Inquiry Questions and Comments

- How does the bag feel?

- What do you see inside the bag? Let's identify the items. What colors do you see? Let's count them.

- What happens when you squeeze it? Do the items move around inside the bag?

- What do you see when you place the bag against the glass of the window?

- What do you see when you place it on a light table?

Home-School Connection

Send directions home with parents, along with the bag the child made in class, to make Squeeze, Sparkle, and Shine bags at home.

Suggested Books

- *Baby Touch and Feel Numbers* by DK Publishing

- *Bright Baby Colors, ABC, and Numbers First Words* by Roger Priddy

- *Brown Rabbit's Shape Book* by Alan Baker

- *First 100 Numbers Colors Shapes (Bright Baby)* by Roger Priddy

- *My Five Senses* by Aliki

- *My Five Senses* by Margaret Miller

- *White Rabbit's Color Book* by Alan Baker

Squishy Sensory Soap

Ages

○ **Infants**

○ **Toddlers**

● **Twos**

STEM Concepts

● **Science** (Physical science, Life science)

● **Technology** (Simple tools)

○ **Engineering**

○ **Math**

Learning Outcomes

Children will explore the physical properties of water and elasticity as they explore the sensory foam bubbles.

Teaching Tips

Bubbles provide the opportunity to study science concepts such as elasticity, surface tension, chemistry, and light. Children will engage in the processes of observation and experimentation by playing with the soapy bubbles and squeezing the memory foam pillow.

Materials

• large, flat plastic container or sensory table; the container should be large enough for a memory foam pillow to fit inside

• dishwashing soap

• water

• tablespoon

• measuring cup

• liquid watercolor paints

• hand mixer or eggbeater

• memory foam pillow

• towels for cleanup

Getting Ready

No additional preparation is needed.

How To

Mix 2–3 tablespoons of dishwashing soap and ¼ cup of water in the plastic container or sensory table. Using a handheld mixer or eggbeater, beat soap mixture until you have light, fluffy soapy water. Place the memory foam pillow in the soapy mixture. Invite the children to press the pillow down into the container or sensory table, allowing it to absorb the soapy water. Place drops of liquid watercolor paint into the soapy mixture and let the children begin playing! The liquid watercolors will blend into a rainbow of colors. The memory pillow will be squishy and fun to squeeze. You can add more soap and water if needed.

Hint: This is a great activity to strengthen fine-motor skills.

Expand the Activity

• Place small plastic animals or toys in the sensory table for children to find and explore.

• Add nontoxic glitter to the soapy water.

Build Vocabulary

soap, soapy, bubbles, mix, colors, squeeze, squish, squishy, pillow

Inquiry Questions and Comments

• Watch as we make our soapy bubbles.

• What colors should we place in the sensory table?

• What colors do you see as you mix the colors together?

• What does the pillow feel like when you squeeze it?

• Does the soapy water come out when you squeeze it?

Home-School Connection

Invite parents to repeat this activity at home by placing dishwashing soap and water in the kitchen sink and allowing children to play in the soapy mixture. Children could also play with plastic storage containers in the soapy water.

Suggested Books

• *Bubble Bath Baby* by Libby Ellis

• *Bubbles, Bubbles* by Kathi Appelt

• *Bubbles, Bubbles* by Sesame Street

• *The Bubble Factory* by Tomie De Paola

• *Bubble Trouble* by Margaret Mahy

• *My Five Senses* by Aliki

• *My Five Senses* by Margaret Miller

Stack Them Up

Ages

○ **Infants**

● **Toddlers**

● **Twos**

STEM Concepts

● **Science** (Physical science)

○ **Technology**

● **Engineering** (Engineering)

● **Math** (Number sense and operations, Measurement)

Learning Outcomes

Children will gain experience building, stacking, and counting. Through this activity, children will learn about physical science and mathematics.

Teaching Tips

Children can use a variety of materials to build structures and practice mathematical skills. Children can use the sturdy red cups for building, stacking, and counting.

Materials

12 red party cups

Getting Ready

No additional preparation is needed.

How To

Place the cups out one by one for children to build and play. If they are building, talk to them about balance, stacking, and gravity. Explore ways they can problem solve to build a higher structure. Count the cups with children as they are building. The red cups are sturdy and can be brought out for play throughout the year.

Hint: Children may also choose to stack all the cups inside the other.

Expand the Activity

- Help the children build a tower with the red cups. Give them a ball and show them how to roll it toward the tower to knock it down. Let the children take turns building the tower and then knocking it down. Reinforce the concepts of building and gravity with the children.

- Give children small plastic toys, such as plastic farm or jungle animals, to add to the play and counting activity.

Build Vocabulary

red cups, build, engineer, stack, height, measurement, gravity, balance, count, numbers, inside, outside

Inquiry Questions and Comments

- Here are twelve red cups to play with today.

- What are you building?

- Let's see how high you can build it. How high do you think you can build it?

- Let's count the cups together.

- What happened to it? That's right. They all fell down.

Home-School Connection

Have parents and children build with red cups at home. Ask them to measure the height and see how high parents and children can build a tower. Have parents tell you the measurement the next day. Graph all the answers.

Suggested Books

- *1, 2, Buckle My Shoe* by Anna Grossnickle Hines

- *Baby Touch and Feel: Colors and Shapes* by DK Publishing

- *Baby Touch and Feel: Numbers* by DK Publishing

- *Bright Baby Colors, ABC, and Numbers* by Roger Priddy

- *Construction* by Sally Sutton

- *First 100 Numbers Colors Shapes (Bright Baby)* by Roger Priddy

- *My Very First Book of Numbers* by Eric Carle

- *White Rabbit's Color Book* by Alan Baker

Swishy Fishy Fun

Ages

○ **Infants**

● **Toddlers**

● **Twos**

STEM Concepts

● **Science** (Physical science, Life science)

○ **Technology**

○ **Engineering**

● **Math** (Measurement)

Learning Outcomes

Children will investigate how gelatin powder changes when water is added to it. They will observe how the texture of it changes from a powder to a liquid to a solid. Children will explore the gelatin mixture with their senses.

Teaching Tips

Gelatin is a protein powder used in many commercial products such as shampoo and cosmetics, and as a thickener in foods such as candy, ice cream, and pudding. Gelatin easily dissolves in hot water and sets to a gel when cooled. Therefore, the physical properties of the gelatin change from a powder to a liquid to a solid.

Materials

• 1 box (4 envelopes) of gelatin

• hot water

• large mixing bowl

• large spoon

• measuring cup

• small plastic bowls or storage containers

• plastic tray or baking sheet

• food coloring or liquid watercolor paints

• essential oils, such as lemon or orange, for flavoring, optional

• medium-size plastic fish (safe for toddlers and easy to wash)

Getting Ready

Day 1: Heat the water.

Day 2: Set out trays on a flat surface.

How To

Day 1: Help the children place gelatin powder in a large mixing bowl. Follow the directions on the box regarding the amounts of hot and cold water to add. The children can help stir the gelatin until dissolved. Add blue food coloring and essential oil flavoring, as desired. Pour into individual bowls and let the children add one plastic toy per bowl. Let the gelatin set in refrigerator overnight.

Day 2: Take the gelatin out of the cups in the morning and place them on a tray. Let the children explore the gelatin with their hands and find their fish.

Hint: Children like fruit flavoring best. Little hands may get sticky, so have wet towels close by. Be sure to closely supervise young children to make sure they don't place small objects in their mouths.

Expand the Activity

For older children, let them mix the gelatin and place the mixture in a glass pie pan. Arrange the fish evenly in the pie pan. After it is firm, cut the mold into six even "pie" pieces. You may need to adjust the fish as the gelatin is getting firm so each child can have at least one fish. Count the pieces of the "fishy pie" before you cut it. Let the children explore!

Build Vocabulary

powder, liquid, solid, mixture, mix, measure, spoon, stir, pour, fish, bowl, gelatin, refrigerate

Inquiry Questions and Comments

- Let's get out all the materials we'll need for Swishy Fishy Fun.

- Let's pour the gelatin into the bowl. It's a powder.

- What happens when we stir the mixture?

- How does it change?

- How does the gelatin change when we add the color to it?

- Let's drop in the fish.

- How does the gelatin feel this morning? It's firm. Yesterday it was liquid. Today it is a solid.

- How does it feel in your hand?

Home-School Connection

Invite parents to make gelatin at home and add fruit to it for dessert or a snack.

Suggested Books

- *Baby Touch and Feel: Splish! Splash!* by DK Publishing

- *Quick as a Cricket* by Audrey Wood and Don Wood

- *Fidgety Fish* by Ruth Galloway

- *Fidgety Fish and Friends* by Ruth Galloway

- *Five Little Ducks* by Annie Kubler and Penny Ives

- *My Five Senses* by Aliki

- *My Five Senses* by Margaret Miller

- *The Rainbow Fish* by Marcus Pfister and J. Alison James

Touch and Feel Box

Ages

- ● **Infants**
- ● **Toddlers**
- ○ **Twos**

STEM Concepts

- ● **Science** (Physical science, Life science)
- ● **Technology** (Simple tools)
- ○ **Engineering**
- ● **Math** (Spatial relationship)

Learning Outcomes

Children will gain awareness of different textures as they explore items through their sense of touch.

Teaching Tips

The sense of touch is one of our five senses. Through tactile exploration, children learn about their sense of touch and the physical properties of different materials.

Materials

- small, sturdy box or shoebox
- variety of textured materials, such as sandpaper, plastic wrap, doubled-sided tape, fake fur, felt, or bubble wrap
- scissors
- electrical tape
- markers
- contact paper
- glue

Getting Ready

Create the sensory box by cutting a hole in the top of the box large enough for children to put their hands through. Cover the edges of the hole with electrical tape. Cut the textured materials to fit the inside of the box. Glue the pieces down, lining the inside of the box, including the inside top of the box. Tape the top on the box using electrical tape and cover the outside of the box with contact paper. Using the markers label the box "Sensory Box." Be sure to leave samples of the materials out so children can explore them prior to placing their hand in the box.

How To

Lay out the different textured materials on a table. Let the children feel the materials and explain how each texture is different. Help children learn the names of the different materials. Let children take turns feeling inside the box. Ask them what they feel and what they like and dislike about the textures.

Hint: You may have some children who do not wish to stick their hands in the box, which is fine. Invite them to explore the materials on a tray. They may want to try the sensory box after watching other children enjoy the fun.

Expand the Activity

- Lift the top off the sensory box and have the children look inside.

- Let the children examine the materials closely with a magnifying glass.

- Using a flashlight, shine the light through the hole in the box.

- Go for a walk outdoors and collect materials that can be used for a second sensory box.

Build Vocabulary

box, top, bottom, hole, touch, feel, smooth, texture, sandpaper, rough, soft, sticky, fur, hands, fingers, senses

Inquiry Questions and Comments

- We're going to create a sensory box. We're going to explore with our senses.

- Here are several different textures for you to feel. This piece is called sandpaper.

- How does it feel? It feels rough.

- How does this feel different from the piece of fur?

- Which texture feels sticky?

- Let's look inside the box and see all the different textures.

Home-School Connection

Invite parents to identify different textures they have in their homes. Kitchens are full of different textures. For example, kitchen towels, wooden spoons, and plastic bowls all have different textures.

Suggested Books

- *Baby Touch and Feel: Animals* by DK Publishing

- *Baby Touch and Feel: Farm* by DK Publishing

- *Baby Touch and Feel: Puppies and Kittens* by DK Publishing

- *Baby Touch and Feel: Wild Animals* by DK Publishing

- *Baby Touch and Feel: Zoo's Who?* By Roger Priddy

- *Don't Touch, It's Hot (Touch and Feel)* by David Algrim and Holli Conger

- *Farm Animals* by Phoebe Dunn

- *Happy Baby Animals* by Roger Priddy

- *My Five Senses* by Aliki

- *My Five Senses* by Margaret Miller

Tummy Time: Discovery Painting

Ages

● **Infants**
○ **Toddlers**
○ **Twos**

STEM Concepts

● **Science** (Physical science)
○ **Technology**
○ **Engineering**
○ **Math**

Learning Outcomes

Children will explore the physical properties of mixing colors as they use their hands to manipulate the paints inside a plastic freezer storage bag.

Teaching Tips

Mixing two or three separate colors together creates a new color.

Materials

• white piece of construction paper
• 3 colors of washable tempera paint
• 1 gallon resealable freezer bag
• scissors
• masking tape or duct tape

Getting Ready

Place drops of tempera paint on the paper. Place the paper in the freezer bag and seal it shut. Place tape on all four sides of the bag and securely tape it to the floor.

How To

Place the baby on a slight incline so the baby can reach the bag. Let the baby explore the bag and manipulate the paint.

Warning: Babies can wiggle out of their tummy time spot, so keep an eye on them. Use a heavy-duty freezer bag and tape it securely to the floor. Tape it on a hard flooring surface rather than carpet.

Expand the Activity

• For older children, tape the bag to a sliding glass door or window and let them play.

• Repeat the activity when the child is old enough to sit in a high chair.

Build Vocabulary

paint, bag, color, mix, hand

Inquiry Questions and Comments

• Look at the colors changing.

• I see you moving your hand on the bag.

• You are making the paint move side to side (or up and down or sideways).

Home-School Connection

Send home paint and a piece of paper with the instructions for how to create the sealed bag. Encourage parents to do this at home or to bring it with them to a restaurant as something for their child to do.

Suggested Books

- *Baby Touch and Feel: Colors and Shapes* by DK Publishing

- *Baby Touch and Feel: Numbers* by DK Publishing

- *Bright Baby Colors, ABC, and Numbers* by Roger Priddy

- *First 100 Numbers Colors Shapes (Bright Baby)* by Roger Priddy

- *Mouse Paint* by Ellen Stoll Walsh

- *My Crayons Talk* by Patricia Hubbard

- *My Very First Book of Numbers* by Eric Carle

- *White Rabbit's Color Book* by Alan Baker

Tummy Time: Sensory Play

Ages

- ● **Infants**
- ○ **Toddlers**
- ○ **Twos**

STEM Concepts

- ● **Science** (Physical science, Life science)
- ○ **Technology**
- ○ **Engineering**
- ○ **Math**

Learning Outcomes

Babies will explore different sensory materials as they strengthen head, neck, and tummy muscles during tummy time.

Teaching Tips

Exploration of sensory materials will promote sensory awareness in babies.

Materials

- balls or soft toys for babies to explore
- tummy time mats

Getting Ready

No additional preparation is needed.

How To

Lay the children down on their tummy time mats. Show them balls or soft toys and let them explore the objects. Sit with the children and talk about what you see them doing as they explore the toy with their senses.

Hint: Introduce a few age-appropriate items that make noise when shaken. Be sure to closely supervise young children to make sure they don't place small objects in their mouths.

Expand the Activity

- When children are able to sit up on their own, roll a ball back and forth with them.
- Add sensory materials, such as wood blocks, plastic baby blocks, or rattles, for them to explore as they get older.

Build Vocabulary

see, touch, feel, smell, hear, bumpy, smooth, shiny, soft

Inquiry Questions and Comments

- Let's shake it and see what we hear.
- Let's touch it and see how it feels.
- I wonder how this feels. It feels . . .
- I see . . . (colors, shapes, and so on).

Home-School Connection

Invite parents to give babies a variety of age-appropriate toys to explore while engaging in tummy time.

Suggested Books

- *Baby Touch and Feel: Animals* by DK Publishing

- *Baby Touch and Feel: Farm* by DK Publishing

- *Baby Touch and Feel: Puppies and Kittens* by DK Publishing

- *Baby Touch and Feel: Wild Animals* by DK Publishing

- *Baby Touch and Feel: Zoo's Who?* By Roger Priddy

- *Don't Touch, It's Hot (Touch and Feel)* by David Algrim and Holli Conger

- *Farm Animals* by Phoebe Dunn

- *Happy Baby Animals* by Roger Priddy

- *My Five Senses* by Aliki

- *My Five Senses* by Margaret Miller

Twig Painting

Ages

○ Infants

● Toddlers

● Twos

STEM Concepts

● **Science** (Physical science, Life science, Earth science)

● **Technology** (Simple tools)

○ **Engineering**

● **Math** (Number sense and operations)

Learning Outcomes

Children will gain a sense of life and earth science as they collect twigs on a nature walk. They will observe and explore the leaves and flowers on plants and trees on their walk.

Teaching Tips

A nature walk is a great opportunity for children to experience the properties of earth science while learning about the parts of trees and plants. Take along a bag to collect the twigs that the children pick up off the ground.

Materials

- liquid tempera paint in fall colors
- small containers for paint
- twigs and branches, about 4–8 inches in length
- magnifying glasses
- white construction paper
- masking tape
- water and paper towels for cleanup

Getting Ready

Place yellow, orange, brown, and green liquid tempera paints in small containers.

How To

Place the collected twigs on a table. Invite the children to touch and feel the twigs. Talk to them about what they see and feel. Model how they can use a magnifying glass to examine the bark of the twigs more closely. Tape one or two small twigs on a white piece of construction paper and give one sheet to each child. Invite the children to dip their fingers into the paint and use finger print marks to add fall leaves around the edges of the twigs.

Hint: You may want to collect twigs ahead of time in case you only find a few on your nature walk. Be sure to closely supervise young children to make sure they don't place small objects in their mouths.

Expand the Activity

- Repeat this activity in the spring and paint with colors representing leaves and flowers.

- Give each child a twig to paint. Place a variety of colors on the table for painting. Once the paint on the twigs has dried, place all the twigs in a jar on the table for the children to enjoy.

Build Vocabulary

twigs, gather, walk, nature, smooth, bumpy, tape, paint, fall, colors, fingerprints

Inquiry Questions and Comments

- We're going to go for a walk and observe the trees and plants. What do you see when you look at the tree? What colors are the leaves?

- Let's pick up some small twigs and place them in the bag.

- What does the twig feel like? Is it smooth or bumpy?

- What does it feel like to dip your finger in the paint?

- How does the paint feel?

- Let's make fingerprints on the paper to look like leaves.

- Do you see your fingerprints? Let's count them.

Home-School Connection

Invite parents to go on a nature walk and collect fallen leaves and twigs and place them in a bowl or a clear jar as a centerpiece.

Suggested Books

- *Are You a Butterfly?* by Judy Allen
- *Are You a Ladybug?* by Judy Allen
- *Bugs* by Andrews McMeel Publishing
- *Counting in the Garden* by Kim Parker
- *I Love Bugs* by Philemon Sturges
- *In the Tall, Tall Grass* by Denise Fleming
- *Mouse Paint* by Ellen Stoll Walsh
- *The Surprise Garden* by Zoe Hall

Twirling Objects

Ages

- ● **Infants**
- ● **Toddlers**
- ○ **Twos**

STEM Concepts

- ● **Science** (Physical science)
- ● **Technology** (Simple tools)
- ● **Engineering** (Engineering)
- ● **Math** (Number sense and operations)

Learning Outcomes

Children will gain an understanding of how magnetic force works as they move the magnetic wand up and down the outside of the sensory bottle. They will observe the objects move as they are pulled by the magnetic force.

Teaching Tips

Magnetism is physical force caused by an electric charge where objects are attracted to (pull) or are repelled from one another.

Materials

- chenille stems cut into different-size pieces
- scissors
- large magnetic wand
- empty, clean plastic water bottle
- decorative duct tape
- funnel

Getting Ready

Cut the chenille stems into a variety of different sizes with the maximum being 3 inches in length. For infants and younger toddlers, create the sensory bottle ahead of time following the instructions in step 1 below.

How To

1. For older toddlers, place the cut pieces of chenille stem on a plastic tray. Have the children play with and sort the pieces. Place a funnel in the top of the water bottle and let the children drop the chenille stems into the bottle. Seal with colorful duct tape.

2. Model how you can make the chenille stems twirl around the bottle with the help of the magnetic wand. The objects with metal in them will "twirl" as the wand moves up and down the side of the bottle.

Hint: Large-handled magnetic wands work better than the smaller, inexpensive ones. The larger wands have more magnetic pull.

Expand the Activity

- Make a separate bottle with other items that have metal in them, such as paper clips, coins, alphabet and number magnets, or small magnetic balls. Collect some items, such as pom-poms or plastic animals, that do not have metal in them. Place all items in the bottle and seal it closed. Using the magnetic wand, have the children observe which items contain metal and which ones do not.

- Invite children to go for a hunt around the room to investigate which items attract or repel the magnetic force of the wand.

Build Vocabulary

magnetic wand, magnet, pull, motion, movement, twirl, chenille stem, scissors, funnel

Inquiry Questions and Comments

- What colors do you see in the bottle?
- Let's move the wand up and down along the side of the bottle. Do you see the chenille stems move?
- What happens when you shake and move the bottle up and down?
- What do you hear?

Home-School Connection

Invite parents to have the children play with magnetic alphabet letters on the outside of the refrigerator or on a cookie sheet.

Suggested Books

- *Baby Touch and Feel: Colors and Shapes* by DK Publishing
- *Bright Baby Colors, ABC, and Numbers* by Roger Priddy
- *First 100 Numbers Colors Shapes (Bright Baby)* by Roger Priddy
- *National Geographic Little Kids First Big Book of Why* by Catherine Hughes
- *Richard Scarry's A Day at the Airport* by Richard Scarry
- *Richard Scarry's Best First Book Ever!* by Richard Scarry
- *Rosie Revere, Engineer* by Andrea Beaty
- *White Rabbit's Color Book* by Alan Baker

Up, Up, and Away: Bubble Play

Ages

○ Infants
● Toddlers
● Twos

STEM Concepts

● **Science** (Physical science, Life science, Earth science)
● **Technology** (Simple tools)
○ **Engineering**
● **Math** (Spatial relationships)

Learning Outcomes

Children will explore the properties of physical, life, and earth sciences as they blow bubbles.

Children will blow the soapy solution through the wands using their breath.

Teaching Tips

A bubble is a thin film of soapy water filled with air. Bubbles can pop for several reasons, including hitting a dry surface, being broken by a strong wind, or having the air inside the bubble evaporate.

Materials

• plastic bucket or pan
• dishwashing soap
• water
• eggbeater
• measuring cup

- measuring spoon

- a variety of bubble wands, purchased or made from string, chenille stems, a flyswatter, plastic berry baskets, slotted spoons, plastic cookie cutters, vegetable strainers, yarn, or wire coat hangers

- glycerin (found in drug stores), optional

- corn syrup, optional

- towels

Getting Ready

No additional preparation is needed.

How To

Place the 1 cup of water and 2 tablespoons of dishwashing soap in the plastic bucket. Beat the mixture with the eggbeater. Dip the wands into the soapy solution. Demonstrate for younger children how to blow into the soapy wand. Describe the bubbles and let the children play. You can add 1–2 tablespoons of either corn syrup or glycerin for a different bubble experience. If you wish to make your own Bubble Wand, see page 66.

Hint: This activity can get messy and is best done outdoors on a sunny day. It's best to make the mixture the day before and let it sit overnight.

Expand the Activity

Make colored bubbles by mixing 1 cup liquid tempera paint, 2 tablespoons of dishwashing soap, and 1 tablespoon of glycerin or ¼ cup corn syrup. Color bubbles can be a bit messy, so be sure that children are wearing painting aprons and use washable paint. If the mixture is too thick, thin it with water. This is a great way to help children learn their colors.

Build Vocabulary

bubbles, soapy solution, wand, flyswatter, plastic berry baskets, slotted spoons, plastic cookie cutters, vegetable strainer, wire coat hanger, pop, clear, float

Inquiry Questions and Comments

- I've got bubbles for us to play with today.

- How does the bubble water feel?

- What do you want to use for a wand?

- What happens as we place the wand in the soapy water? Use your breath to blow the bubbles.

- What happens when the wind blows the bubble?

- Let's watch it and see how far it will float in the sky.

Home-School Connection

Invite parents to repeat the activity at home using household items.

Suggested Books

- *Bubble Bath Baby* by Libby Ellis

- *The Bubble Factory* by Tomie De Paola

- *Bubbles, Bubbles* by Kathi Appelt

- *Bubbles, Bubbles* by Sesame Street

- *Bubble Trouble* by Margaret Mahy

- *My Five Senses* by Aliki

- *My Five Senses* by Margaret Miller

Water Toy Slide

Ages

○ **Infants**

○ **Toddlers**

● **Twos**

STEM Concepts

● **Science** (Physical science)

● **Technology** (Simple tools)

● **Engineering** (Engineering)

● **Math** (Number sense, Measurement)

Learning Outcomes

Children will begin to learn about gravity as they experience how objects travel down an inclined plane.

Teaching Tips

Gravity is the natural force that tends to cause physical objects to move toward each other; it is the force that causes objects to fall toward Earth. The slope of an inclined plane will increase or decrease the speed of a falling object.

Materials

• 2 foam pool noodles

• knife or box cutter

• electrical tape

• small cars or rolling objects

• chair or small footstool

• plastic container or bucket

• water

Getting Ready

Using a knife or box cutter, cut the pool noodles in half lengthwise.

How To

To construct the slide, tape the rounded or back side of the noodles together side by side. This will allow two rolling objects to slide down the middle of each noodle. Tape together several pool noodles if you want a larger or wider slide. Place the noodle slide on an incline, using a chair or small footstool. It should be high enough for children to reach without stretching. They should be able to easily watch the objects roll down the slide. Modify the height for children as needed.

Place a bucket or plastic container with water at the bottom of the slide. Let children drop objects down the slide to observe how gravity and incline planes work.

Hint: Be sure to closely supervise young children to make sure they don't place small objects in their mouths. Additionally, closely supervise children around water.

Expand the Activity

• Count how long it takes for the small cars or toys to roll down the slide. Invite children to make predictions about which cars will go down the slide fastest. Let children have races to see which toy goes faster. Document the children's predictions and the results of the race.

• For outdoor fun, take the noodle slide outside. Give the children a small bucket or pitcher of water and let them pour water down the slide. Tape objects in the middle of the slide for the water to go over or create a dam to block the water from spilling down.

Build Vocabulary

roll, slide, incline, race, speed, fast, faster, bucket, chair, higher, gravity, construct, build

Inquiry Questions and Comments

- Let's construct the noodle slide.
- What happened when we cut the noodle in half?
- How many pieces do we have now?
- We're going to tape the back to secure the two pieces together. Let's place one end of the slide on the chair.
- Which end of the noodle is higher?
- What do you think will happen when we place the toy here?
- Why do you think it will roll down the slide?

Home-School Connection

Invite parents to work with their child to create an inclined plane at home using a cereal box or other flat container. Encourage them to find objects that roll, such as an orange or ping pong ball, and roll the object down the inclined plane.

Suggested Books

- *Baby Touch and Feel: Splish! Splash!* by DK Publishing
- *Baby Polar Bear* by Aubrey Lang and Wayne Lynch
- *Bright Baby Colors, ABC, & Numbers First Words* by Roger Priddy
- *First 100 Words (Bright Baby)* by Roger Priddy
- *My Five Senses* by Aliki
- *My Five Senses* by Margaret Miller
- *Sally in the Sand* by Stephen Huneck
- *Richard Scarry's Best First Book Ever!* by Richard Scarry
- *Tacky the Penguin* by Helen Lester

What's the Scoop?

Ages

- ● Infants
- ● Toddlers
- ○ Twos

STEM Concepts

- ● **Science** (Physical science, Life science)
- ● **Technology** (Simple tools)
- ○ **Engineering**
- ● **Math** (Number sense and operations)

Learning Outcomes

Children will gain experience with number sense and operations as they scoop and transfer items into containers using a variety of simple tools. Children will also practice fine-motor skills.

Teaching Tips

Number sense and operations is developed as children count and sort items using a variety of simple tools.

Materials

- 3–4 small plastic containers
- items for transferring, such as pom-poms, beads, beans, small sponge pieces, counting bears
- tools for scooping, such as an ice cream scoop, melon scoop, large spoon, tongs, measuring spoons, or coffee scoop
- ice cube tray or muffin tin

Getting Ready

Collect items for scooping and transferring and place them in separate plastic containers.

How To

Show young children how to use the scooping utensils. Model how to transfer the materials from the plastic containers into either an ice cube tray or muffin tin cup. Talk with the children about the process of scooping and transferring items. Count the number of scoops and transfers as the children engage in the process.

Hint: Use small scooping utensils with short handles for young children. Be sure to closely supervise young children to make sure they don't place small objects in their mouths.

Expand the Activity

- Let the children practice transferring colored water from a container into an ice cube tray using an eyedropper.
- Let children scoop and transfer plastic colored eggs into a bucket of water using a large slotted spoon. Be sure to seal the plastic eggs closed with colored duct tape.

Build Vocabulary

scoop, transfer, hold, ice cube tray, muffin tin, pom-poms, beads, counting bears, spoons, hands, fingers

Inquiry Questions and Comments

- Let's practice scooping our items. We have pom-poms, beads, and counting bears to scoop.

- Place the scoop here in the muffin cup. Wow, look at you transferring the pom-poms!

- I see you using your fingers too!

- Let's count the scoops—one, two, three.

- Which kind of scoop do you like?

Home-School Connection

Invite parents to let children practice scooping and transferring items at home.

Suggested Books

- *Baby Touch and Feel: Colors and Shapes* by DK Publishing

- *Baby Touch and Feel: Numbers* by DK Publishing

- *Bright Baby Colors, ABC, and Numbers* by Roger Priddy

- *First 100 Numbers Colors Shapes (Bright Baby)* by Roger Priddy

- *My Very First Book of Numbers* by Eric Carle

- *White Rabbit's Color Book* by Alan Baker

Wind Chime

Ages

○ **Infants**

○ **Toddlers**

● **Twos**

STEM Concepts

● **Science** (Physical science, Earth science)

● **Technology** (Simple tools)

● **Engineering** (Engineering)

● **Math** (Shapes and spatial relationships, Mathematical reasoning)

Learning Outcomes

Children will learn the parts of wind chimes and properties of the wind. They will learn how to use recycled materials to create open-ended art.

Teaching Tips

A wind chime is made of materials that hang loosely from a secure base. Several pieces of material are hung as the tubing with another material hung as the clapper. When the wind blows, they move and make noise. Recycled materials can be used to engineer a wind chime. This is a great way to introduce young children to earth science and a creative way to recycle materials.

Materials

• pieces of driftwood, flat pieces of wood, small embroidery hoops, an empty potato chip or yogurt container for the base

• variety of items to hang from the base, such as beads, bells, driftwood, pieces of bamboo, keys, seashells, buttons

• drill

• eye hooks

• twine or nylon fishing line

• scissors

• large buttons

• long pieces of colorful ribbons, optional

Getting Ready

Collect small items to hang from the wind chime. Drill holes in any items that do not already have a hole in them. Screw eye hooks into any wood pieces. Cut the twine or nylon fishing line into varying lengths. Ask parents to donate materials to use in this activity. Use your imagination on how to use recycled materials!

How To

Let the children select the items they want on their wind chime and help string them on the twine or fishing line. Be creative in what children can use to create their wind chimes. Talk to the children about recycling materials and protecting the environment. Have children help or hold items as you knot and secure the items. Tie the items at different lengths to the base. Hang the base outdoors or from the ceiling of your learning environment using fishing line.

Hint: Large buttons are great for securing the fishing line to the base. Knot the fishing line through the holes in the button and then secure the button on the base with an additional knot.

Be sure to closely supervise young children to make sure they don't place small objects in their mouths.

Expand the Activity

Create wind chimes with like items such as all seashells, wood pieces, or kitchen utensils. Like items will help support specific STEM curricular themes.

Build Vocabulary

wind chime, wind, hang, create, wood, base, beads, bells, seashells, ribbons, knot, secure, tree, blow, move

Inquiry Questions and Comments

- We're going to create a wind chime. What items do you want to put on yours?

- Once we're done, we'll hang it from the tree outdoors.

- What do you see when you look at the wind chime?

- Do you see the ribbons moving in the wind?

- What do you think will happen when the wind blows hard?

- What sounds does it make?

- Do you hear the bells ringing?

Home-School Connection

Purchase or make a wind chime at home and hang it outdoors. Talk with the children about what they hear and see when the wind blows and the chime makes sounds.

Suggested Books

- *My Five Senses* by Aliki

- *My Five Senses* by Margaret Miller

- *What Is the Weather Today?* by Rebecca Bondor

- *What Makes the Seasons?* by Megan Montague Cash

- *Whistle for Willie* by Ezra Jack Keats

- *The Wind Blew* by Pat Hutchins

- *A Windy Day in Spring* by Charles Ghigna and Laura Watson

Glossary

Absorption: The process by which one substance takes up another substance or is absorbed.

Analyzing: The process of considering information and data gathered during an experiment.

Balance: The even distribution of weight enabling an object or a person to remain steady and upright.

Buoyancy: The ability or tendency of an object to float in either water, air, or some other type of fluid.

Bridge: A structure built over a river, road, or railway that allows people and vehicles to move across an open space. Bridges are designed to hold weight and need anchors on either end to help support the deck.

Cause and effect: The relationship between actions or events, where one is the result of the other or others. The cause is why something happens and the effect is what happens as a result of the why.

Classification: The process of comparing and contrasting like and unlike items.

Density: Objects, including liquids, are made up of atoms and molecules, each of which is a certain mass and size. Liquids sink or float depending on the density (mass or size) of the molecules in the object or material.

Design: To make decisions and plan something that is to be built or created.

Documentation: The collection of materials or data to prove something or to provide evidence.

Earth science: The study of observing and exploring the properties of earth materials such as soil, water, air, and rocks.

Engineering: Planning and building something in order to solve a problem.

Evidence: The data gathered from observing or testing.

Examine: To look at something closely in order to learn more about it or to gather information.

Experiment: A test or an investigation performed to answer a specific question.

Explore: To investigate and examine.

Force: Something that causes a change in motion of an object.

Gravity: The natural force that tends to cause physical objects to move toward each other; the force that causes objects to fall toward Earth.

Height: The distance from the bottom to the top of a person or thing or how tall something is.

Incline: To lean or slope.

Investigate: To gather information or data by testing and observing.

Inquiry: The act of asking questions in order to gather information or examine facts.

Life science: The study of the properties and characteristics of living things.

Magnetic pull: A physical force caused by an electric charge where objects are attracted to (pull) or repelled from one another.

Magnetism: The property of attracting certain metals.

Mathematics: The study of numbers, equations, functions, algebra, geometry, and their relationships.

Motion: The act or process of moving.

Observation: Using your senses to gather information or data.

Oobleck: A non-Newtonian fluid made of water and cornstarch, which when mixed has properties that are both liquid and solid.

Physical science: The study of characteristics and physical properties of nonliving objects and of solid and liquid materials, and changes in objects and materials.

Plasticity: A period of brain development where the brain is susceptible to pruning and stimulation.

Properties: A special quality or characteristic of an object or set of objects that can be observed.

Record: Method in which data and/or information is archived or stored.

Science: The study of observing, investigating, and exploring how the world works.

Scientific inquiry: The process of observing, investigating, classifying, describing, and experimenting.

Senses: The body's natural tools (touch, taste, hearing, sight, and smell) for gathering information.

Simple machines: Devices designed by humans to make certain tasks easier. Simple machines include inclined planes, wedges, pulleys, levers, wheels and axles, and screws.

Simple tools: Tools designed by humans to make work easier. Simple tools include scissors, tweezers, tongs, magnifying glasses, scales and balances, measuring utensils, and knives.

STEM: An acronym for science, technology, engineering, and math.

Tactile: An experience that is connected to the sense of touch.

Technology: The application of scientific knowledge to invent useful things or to solve problems.

Temperature: How hot or cold something is.

Texture: How something looks or feels.

Volume: The amount of space that a substance or object occupies.

Weight: How heavy or light something is.

Width: The distance from one side to the other or how wide something is.

Books That Promote STEM Learning

1, 2, Buckle My Shoe by Anna Grossnickle Hines

Apples and Pumpkins by Anne Rockwell
The Apple Pie Tree by Zoe Hall
Are You an Ant? by Judy Allen
Are You a Bee? by Judy Allen
Are You a Butterfly? by Judy Allen
Are You a Ladybug? by Judy Allen
Autumn Leaves by Ken Robbins
Awesome Autumn by Bruce Goldstone

Baby Polar Bear by Aubrey Lang and Wayne Lynch
Baby's Animal Friends by Phoebe Dunn
Baby's Shapes by Karen Katz
Baby Touch and Feel: Animals by DK Publishing
Baby Touch and Feel: Colors and Shapes by DK Publishing
Baby Touch and Feel: Farm by DK Publishing
Baby Touch and Feel: Numbers by DK Publishing
Baby Touch and Feel: Puppies and Kittens by DK Publishing
Baby Touch and Feel: Splish! Splash! by DK Publishing
Baby Touch and Feel: Trucks by DK Publishing
Baby Touch and Feel: Wild Animals by DK Publishing
Baby Touch and Feel: Zoo's Who? By Roger Priddy
Barnyard Dance by Sandra Boynton
Bartholomew and the Oobleck by Dr. Seuss
Big and Little: Things That Go by Rebecca Bondor
Big Board First 100 Machines by Roger Priddy
Big Book of Things That Go by DK Publishing
Big Red Barn by Margaret Wise Brown
Blue Hat, Green Hat by Sandra Boynton
Boats by Anne Rockwell
Boats Board Book by Byron Barton
Bridges: Amazing Structures to Design, Build, and Test by Carol A. Johmann
Bright Baby Animals by Roger Priddy
Bright Baby Colors, ABC, and Numbers by Roger Priddy
Bright Baby Colors, ABC, and Numbers First Words by Roger Priddy
Bright Baby Touch and Feel Baby Animals by Roger Priddy
Brown Rabbit's Shape Book by Alan Baker
Bubble Bath Baby by Libby Ellis
The Bubble Factory by Tomie De Paola
Bubbles, Bubbles by Kathi Appelt
Bubbles, Bubbles by Sesame Street
Bubble Trouble by Margaret Mahy
The Bugliest Bugs by Carol Diggory Shield
Bugs by Andrews McMeel Publishing
Bugs! Bugs! Bugs! by Bob Barner
Butterflies by Karen Shapiro

Circus Shapes by Stuart J. Murphy
Construction by Sally Sutton
Counting in the Garden by Kim Parker
Counting Kisses: A Kiss and Read Book by Karen Katz
Counting 1 to 20 by Rebecca Bondor

Dancing Feet by Lindsey Craig
Dig Dig Digging by Margaret Mayo
Dinosaur Bones by Bob Barner
Don't Touch, It's Hot (Touch and Feel) by David Algrim and Holli Conger

Eating the Alphabet: Fruits and Vegetables from A to Z by Lois Ehlert

Farm Animals by Phoebe Dunn
Fidgety Fish by Ruth Galloway
Fidgety Fish and Friends by Ruth Galloway
First 100 Numbers Colors Shapes (Bright Baby) by Roger Priddy
First 100 Trucks (Bright Baby) by Roger Priddy
First 100 Words (Bright Baby) by Roger Priddy
Five Little Ducks by Annie Kubler and Penny Ives
Food from Farms by Nancy Dickmann
From the Garden: A Counting Book about Growing Food by Michael Dahl and Todd Ouren

From Head to Toe (board book) by Eric Carle

Fuzzy Fuzzy Fuzzy! (Boynton Board Books) by Sandra Boynton

Giraffes Can't Dance by Giles Andreae and Guy Parker-Rees

Goodnight, Goodnight, Construction Site by Sherri Duskey Rinker and Tom Lichtenheld

Goodnight Moon by Margaret Wise Brown

Goodnight Moon 123 Board Book: A Counting Book by Margaret Wise Brown and Clement Hurd

Gray Rabbit's 1, 2, 3 by Alan Baker

Grouchy Ladybug by Eric Carle

Growing Frogs by Vivian French

Happy Baby Animals by Roger Priddy

Hello, Bugs! by Smriti Prasadam and Emily Bolam

Hello Ocean by Pam Muñoz Ryan

Hippos Go Berserk! by Sandra Boynton

How Are You Peeling? by Saxton Freymann and Joost Elffers

How a House Is Built by Gail Gibbons

How Many Snails? by Paul Giganti and Donald Crews

Iggy Peck, Architect by Andrea Beaty and David Roberts

I Love Bugs by Philemon Sturges

In the Tall, Tall Grass by Denise Fleming

In the Sea by David Elliot

Let's Count Trucks: A Fun Kids' Counting Book for Toddler Boys and Children Age 2 to 5 by Alina Niemi

Little Blue Truck by Alice Schertle and Jill McElmurry

Little Blue Truck Leads the Way by Alice Schertle and Jill McElmurry

The Little Gardener by Jan Gerardi

The Little Mouse, the Red Ripe Strawberry, and the Big Hungry Bear by Don Wood and Audrey Wood

Look at That Building by Scot Ritchie

Magnificent Monarchs by Linda Glaser

Monarch Butterfly by Gail Gibbons

Monarch and Milkweed by Helen Frost

Moo Baa La La La by Sandra Boynton

Mouse Paint by Ellen Stoll Walsh

Mouse Shapes by Ellen Stoll Walsh

Mrs. Wishy-Washy's Farm by Joy Cowley

My Big Animal Book by Roger Priddy

My Big Truck Book by Roger Priddy

My Crayons Talk by Patricia Hubbard

My First Baby Animals: Let's Find Our Favorites! by DK Publishing

My First Body by DK Publishing

My Five Senses by Aliki

My Five Senses by Margaret Miller

My Hands by Aliki

My Truck Is Stuck by Kevin Lewis and Daniel Kirk

My Very First Book of Animal Sounds by Eric Carle

My Very First Book of Food by Eric Carle

My Very First Book of Numbers by Eric Carle

National Geographic Little Kids First Big Book of Animals by Catherine Hughes

National Geographic Little Kids First Big Book of Bugs by Catherine Hughes

National Geographic Little Kids First Big Book of Space by Catherine Hughes

National Geographic Little Kids First Big Book of Why by Catherine Hughes

Not a Box by Antoinette Portis

Old Macdonald Had a Farm by Child's Play and Pam Adams

One Big Building: A Counting Book about Construction by Michael Dahl and Todd Ouren

One Duck Stuck: A Mighty Ducky Counting Book by Phyllis Root and Jane Chapman

On the Seashore by Anna Milbourne

Open the Barn Door by Christopher Santoro

Pat the Bunny by Dorothy Kunhardt

Pete the Cat: Old MacDonald Had a Farm by James Dean

Planting a Rainbow by Lois Ehlert

Quick as a Cricket by Audrey Wood and Don Wood

Rain by Manya Stojic
The Rainbow Fish by Marcus Pfister and J. Alison James
Rainy Day by Emma Haughton
Richard Scarry's A Day at the Airport by Richard Scarry
Richard Scarry's Best First Book Ever by Richard Scarry
Roadwork by Sally Sutton
Roar: A Big-Mouthed Book of Sounds! by Jonathan Litton and Fhiona Galloway
Roar! A Noisy Counting Book by Pamela Duncan Edwards and Henry Cole
Roar, Roar, Baby! by Karen Katz
Roaring Rockets by Tony Milton and Ant Parker
Roll, Slope, and Slide: A Book about Ramps by Michael Dahl
Rosie's Walk by Pat Hutchins
Rosie Revere, Engineer by Andrea Beaty and David Roberts

Sally at the Farm by Stephen Huneck
Sally in the Forest by Stephen Huneck
Sally in the Sand by Stephen Huneck
Sally in the Snow by Stephen Huneck
Shapes by Justine Smith and Jill Ackerman
Shapes, Shapes, Shapes by Tana Hoban
Splash by Ann Jonas
Sunflower House by Eve Bunting
The Surprise Garden by Zoe Hall

Tacky the Penguin by Helen Lester and Lynn Munsinger
Tap Tap Bang Bang by Emma Garcia
Ten Little Ladybugs by Melanie Gerth and Laura Huliska-Beith
The Tiny Seed by Eric Carle
Tip Tip Dig Dig by Emma Garcia
Toot Toot Beep Beep by Emma Garcia

Under the Sea by Anna Milbourne

The Very Hungry Caterpillar by Eric Carle

Way Deep in the Deep Blue Sea by Jan Peck
What Is the Weather Today? by Rebecca Bondor
What Makes the Seasons? by Megan Montague Cash
Wheels on the Bus by Jerry Smath
When I Build with Blocks by Niki Alling
Where Butterflies Grow by Joanne Ryder
Where Is Baby's Beach Ball? by Karen Katz
Whistle for Willie by Ezra Jack Keats
White Rabbit's Color Book by Alan Baker
Who Lives Here? A Lift-the-Flap Book by Paula Croyle and Heather Brown
Who Sank the Boat? by Pamela Allen
The Wind Blew by Pat Hutchins
A Windy Day in Spring by Charles Ghigna and Laura Watson
The World's Most Amazing Bridges by Michael Hurley

Zoom, Rocket, Zoom! by Margaret Mayo
Zoom, Zoom, Baby! by Karen Katz

Index of Activities by STEM Concept

Engineering

Math

Index of Activities by Age

References

Barbre, Jean. 2012. *Foundations for Responsive Caregiving Infants, Toddlers and Twos.* St. Paul, MN: Redleaf Press.

Copple, Carol, and Sue Bredekamp, eds. 2009. *Developmentally Appropriate Practice in Early Childhood Programs Serving Children from Birth through Age 8.* 3rd ed. Washington, DC: National Association for the Education of Young Children.

Dodge, Diane Trister, Sherrie Rudick, and Kai-leé Berke. 2006. *Creative Curriculum for Infant, Toddlers, and Twos.* 2nd ed. Washington, DC: Teaching Strategies.

Epstein, A. 2007. *The Intentional Teacher: Choosing the Best Strategies for Young Children's Learning.* Washington, DC: National Association for the Education of Young Children.

Gerber, Bence, and Lisa Sunbury, eds. 2012. "Magda Gerber's RIE Philosophy—Basic Principles." *Magda Gerber, Seeing Babies with New Eyes.* www:magnagerber.org/blog/magda-gerbers-rie-philosophy-basic-principles.

Gerber, Magda. 2016. "Magda Quotes." *Magda Gerber, Seeing Babies with New Eyes.* Accessed January 27. www.magdagerber.org/magda-quotes.html.

Henderson, Anne T., and Karen L. Mapp. 2002. *A New Wave of Evidence: The Impact of School, Family, and Community Connections on Student Achievement.* www.sedl.org/connections/resources/evidence.pdf.

NAEYC (National Association for the Education of Young Children). 2012. "Technology and Interactive Media as Tools in Early Childhood Programs Serving Children from Birth through Age 8." A joint position statement issued by NAEYC and the Fred Rogers Center for Early Learning and Children's Media at Saint Vincent College. http://www.naeyc.org/content/technology-and-young-children.

National Science Foundation. 2015. *Women, Minorities, and Persons with Disabilities in Science and Engineering.* National Center for Science and Engineering Statistics: Directorate for Social, Behavioral and Economic Sciences. https://www.nsf.gov/statistics/2015/nsf15311/digest/nsf15311-digest.pdf.

NEA (National Education Association). 2015. "Science, Technology, Engineering & Math (STEM)." Accessed December 30. www.nea.org/home/stem.html.

———. 2016. "An Educator's Guide to the 'Four Cs': Preparing 21st Century Students for a Global Society." Accessed March 18. http://www.nea.org/tools/52217.htm.

NGSS (Next Generation Science Standards). 2015. "About NGSS." Accessed December 30. www.nextgenscience.org.

Seitz, Hilary. 2008. "The Power of Documentation in the Early Childhood Classroom." *Young Children,* 63 (March): 88–93.